The following stories take place on the lands of the Arakwal,
Minjungbal, and Wiyabul people of the Bundjalung Nation.
We acknowledge them as the Traditional Owners of the
unceded Country on which we live and grow and recognize their
continuing connection to land, waters, and culture. We thank
them for caring for this rainforest and its ecosystems for thousands
of years, and we pay our respects to Elders past and present.

MOTHER
the
MOUNTAIN

The Art of Living with Nature

MOTHER *the* MOUNTAIN

The Art of Living with Nature

———

ANASTASIA & JULIA VANDERBYL

DK | Penguin Random House

Publisher Mike Sanders
Senior Editor Alexander Rigby
Art Director William Thomas
Designer Joanna Price
Photography Anne, Julia, and Anastasia Vanderbyl
Proofreaders Emma Chance, Lisa Starnes
Indexer Beverlee Day

First American Edition, 2023
Published in the United States by DK Publishing
1745 Broadway, 20th Floor, New York, NY 10019

Library of Congress Catalog Number: 2023931913
ISBN: 978-0-7440-8538-9

DK books are available at
special discounts when purchased
in bulk for sales promotions, premiums,
fund-raising, or educational use. For details,
contact SpecialSales@dk.com

Images © Anne, Julia, and Anastasia Vanderbyl
except p91 © David Hancock / Alamy Stock Photo

Printed and bound in China

For the curious
www.dk.com

MIX
Paper | Supporting
responsible forestry
FSC™ C018179

This book was made with Forest
Stewardship Council ™ certified
paper – one small step in DK's
commitment to a sustainable future.
For more information go to
www.dk.com/our-green-pledge

This book is dedicated to those who came before and
those who will come after. To the carers of this earth:
the seed carriers, nurturers, growers, and storytellers.

To our dad, who passed these seeds of care into our hands,
and to our mum, who showed us how to sow them.

Introduction

There is a valley held between two mountains. We live in the folds of its rainforest gullies, cradled by the ridges that rise to the cliff faces above. As children, these mountains marked the edge of our world. We grew in their gaze and learned to trace the dance of the seasons across their faces.

The smallest mountain sits to the south, its wide chalky cliff face is the edge of an ancient volcano caldera. It faces us, acting as a sundial—its shadows shifting to tell us the time of day and the time of year. In the wet season, the sun illuminates the hard rhyolite cliffs, and the monsoonal mist sculpts the tree line. In the dry season, the soft pink light fades as the day turns to night. Its stone is the last place the sun hits. Since we were kids, we've called him *Father the Mountain*.

Beside it stands the tallest mountain in the area, painted with different layers of rainforest. At the very top, there are two bald rocks, and from here you can see the whole world. During heavy summer storms, a waterfall forms at this spot and rushes over the cliffs, flowing into a stream that slowly winds down to us. We have always called her *Mother the Mountain*.

Before we were born, when our brother first learned to speak, he told our parents he came from these mountains. He pointed to the cliff faces and said that there, he had two sisters waiting.

This landscape holds us. It nurtures us with its touch, raising us among the chaos and symbiosis of all things: the snakes, birds, insects, soil, waters, grand trees, and tangled rainforest plants. In this connection we learned to exist. The seasons taught us that all life is cyclical, that what has gone will always come again. The land grew as an extension of ourselves, and we learned to know the plants, stones, and trees like our own skin. We saw that our place in the grand and beautiful web of nature is inconceivably small, but every connection and action can hold so much magnitude. As each new day passes, we understand this a little more. The seasons swirl around us, the mountains hold our little valley, and slowly, we begin to know our place within nature.

Most of all, we are learning the immense significance held in each pebble and seed. In each small part of nature there are the stories of those who have come before and the potential of those who will come next. We are learning that our lives can be gracefully carved within this web, harmonious alongside all creatures. The histories of those who have cared for this rainforest for millennia are woven into the fabric of its interconnection. We feel it is our honor to continue this care, to nurture and heal the land that will also heal us.

In this land's long history, our story is only a flicker. It began with our grandparents—two Dutch immigrants who were some of the first hippies to move to these hills, leaving their world behind them. Together, they planted endless tropical fruit trees, sowing the seeds for the life we live today. Mango, banana, jaboticaba, lychee, and avocado trees are spread over every hill. In their reaching arms and nourishing fruit we are graced with the actions of those before us.

On the highest hill at the very top of the farm, there is an old avocado tree. Its leaves catch the wind, and it stands in gravelly soil that is fine enough to channel the heavy rains that fall in the summer. All water flows down from here, and the old tree's roots stay dry and nourished, its leaves aired, its fruit full and creamy. We often think of our grandparents, standing on this hill as a young couple looking out over the farm and thinking, *this is a good place to live.*

They planted this avocado tree all those years ago, and still, the gravity of their actions reach toward us through time. On a winter's night, this hill is the best place to watch the moon rise over the horizon. We climb up through the tangle of fruit trees and patches of rainforest and reach the old tree's welcome arms. As we pluck its fruit, we feel rooted as deep in the earth as the avocado tree. We feel the presence of our dad as a child, wandering these hills, learning. He would adventure through the valleys barefoot, navigating with the touch of each twisting tree trunk or river stone, knowing their presence to mark a different route. Up high on the edge

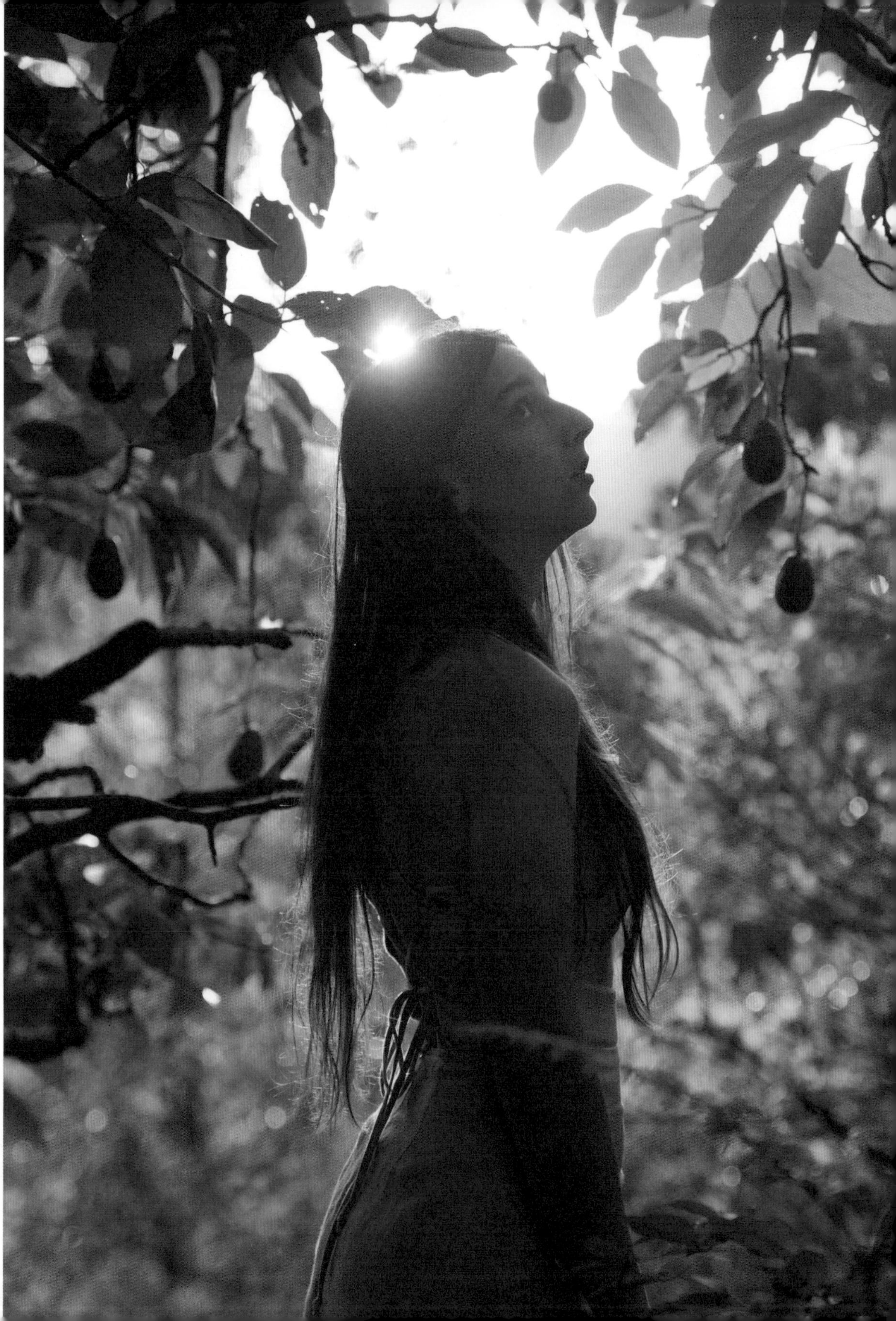

of the craters he would visit the banana farmers. He searched for crystals and snakes between the endless banana plants, collecting stories from the farmers who took this barefoot boy under their wings. Deep in the valleys, beside the winding creeks, he built grand treehouses from vines and fallen trees. His wonder remained even as he grew to become a banana farmer, learning from the old men below the cliff faces. Using just his hands and the learnings of his salvaged jungle treehouse, he became a builder, a woodsman, a man of the trees. To this day, we look to this way of learning—the awe of all things, the wisdom of not knowing—and find this ability to grow within ourselves.

On one of the tallest plateaus in this caldera, the twisting streams meet to form one grand waterfall. The water spills like silk draped over the cliff's edge, the never-ending movement catching the light. Our parents met at the edge of this stream, their stories converging like the soft, shifting waters.

Finding home in each other, they soon became carers for this land, etching their memories into the valleys. On the highest hill, beside the old avocado tree, they planted another. It would grow to watch down on us for years to come. They built a shack on the ancient creek bed, crafted from junk: old doors, forest logs, corrugated iron, and hardwood from the banana plantations. Orchards and sprawling gardens spread outward from their tiny shack, and slowly—as they learned to fell trees and carve them into beams and rafters—a home emerged. This is the place where we grew, sheltered in the beauty of this home under the shadow of the mountain.

We picked fruit with our parents, harvesting the tropical abundance to sell together at the markets. Before we could walk, we would crawl to a macadamia tree, tracing its hardened roots. Our small hands would collect the nuts, learning to crack them open between two rocks. We watched the seasons shift as we lay beneath the forest's canopy. In the soft streams, we sat among the stillness of the rocks, collected mangoes dispersed at our feet, the bright flesh dripping down our chins. Our parents were always building something; making a shack from trees to spend the hot season camping, crafting old windows into a chicken pen, or constructing a cabin entirely from salvaged wood. Learning from this combination of creative and traditional skills, we began to see art in everything. Watching our dad fell a tree and use it to create the beams, rafters, and floorboards for our house. Seeing our mum collect glass from demolition sites and from it, create a grand leadlight window that frames the forest in its gaze. Every element of our childhood in the rainforest was centered around art. The light highlighting the hills like golden brushstrokes. The forests adorned with vibrant fruits. Our character-full family home, built from collected materials. The dance of the seasons. The passing of time.

We left for the city to become artists, to learn our crafts and pursue creative careers. Leaving the valley behind us, we traveled the world and saw mountains, landscapes, cities, and ways of being that left us yearning for more. These experiences let us reflect on our own ways of life, of learning and interacting with the world. In each new city, we had a habit of climbing to the highest hill—

just as we did at home—to look out over the landscape and understand the waters as they flow, from which direction the storms come, and where the moon rises.

We always knew we would return to the nurturing care of the valley. We knew the fruit would still ripen, the creeks would still wane with the seasons, and the mountains would always welcome us home. Our dad suddenly died, and all at once, the landscape's embrace was the only constant amid the forever whirling movement of grief. We returned to the valley to support our mum, and we soon realized the forest could nurture us too. We saw our dad in everything: from the coarse cliffs carved like his jagged nose, to the vines woven with his stories and the hillsides latticed with the tracks of his childhood. The sheep that we grew up alongside still came to his herding call. We learned to mimic his voice, and our own calls now echo through the hills. We climbed that big hill to the avocado trees and planted one of our own, watching the sun set and the moon rise as they always have.

We found that in caring for the land, we were able to heal. By planting trees and nourishing the earth, we in turn found so much hope and new life in everything around us, in each seed sprouting and fern unfurling. A huge family of ducks, chickens, goats, and sheep grew around us. Their joy, innocence, and wonder filled our days, and we learned to see the world through their eyes. We saw that nature is balance—an eternal, intricate, and beautiful balance of all Earth's systems working together. With the animal's help, we found that we can regenerate the earth and find peace within ourselves.

We lived as artists, farmers, makers, and growers. In this simple life in the rainforest, we learned more than we could ever have imagined. We discovered the connection of all things and found our place within the immensity of nature. By working with our hands, we found pleasure and art in everything around us. When we put our energy into the land, immersing all our being into the earth that nurtures us, we felt purpose. In this journey of transformation, we have learned to connect, to create, and to care. We felt the strength of being needed and the meaning that giving brings. We felt happiness.

These lessons haven't all been easy, and since our return, we've faced hardships. The valley has seen drought and fires, unimaginable rains, landslides, and floods. Seeing these landscapes shift and falter during this time of significant change has taught us resilience. We've seen the rivers go dry, then burst their banks. They've changed paths, only to return. From these lessons, we've learned to flow like water, to shift and swirl with the seasons and with ourselves. Mostly, we've learned the importance of protecting nature and helping her return back to health. In regeneration and resilience, there is hope.

What follows are the lessons and teachings of nature that we have found here in our rainforest home: a sharing of knowledge, skills, and stories. Our time nestled in these gullies has taught us a lot, but most of all, we have remembered a way of living that is both simple and profound all at once. It is the art of living with nature.

PART I

CONNECTION

"The food that fed us grew from a seed to a vegetable in our hands. Seasons guided us, and we became the landscape. In this connection, we healed."

The Circularity
of Nature

I let the landscape whisper to me,
the landscape that holds me in her arms.

She tells me that I am the mountain;
sit still and strong and let the seasons pass over me.
To watch twelve moons rise over my ridges,
and evolve with their cycles.

She tells me that I am a rainforest;
I am delicate and strong.
To see the vines and snakes entwined in wholeness,
shaped by growth and decay, summer and winter, life and death.

She tells me that I am a stream;
and I will move on, I will flow and change,
burst my banks and run dry,
but I will always return.

RAISED BY THE RAINFOREST

In each season of our lives, we climbed the mountain. At the end of the valley it stood, shaped from ancient volcanic magma, forever still in time. Every ridge leads to her base. Like veins, creeks wind from the cliff tops to the ocean.

We mapped the secret path through the forgotten trails to the rainforest's edge and beyond. Beginning in the banana plantations, there was danger of becoming lost in the geometrical labyrinth of tracks. The old overgrown paths led to the rainforest's edge. Once inside the forest, the heat of the sun was blocked by broad leaves and palm fronds. We twisted with the vines, crawled over fallen trees, and climbed cliff faces, slowly getting higher. Following ledges of the cliffs, we clutched the ancient rock wall between our fingers. *Don't look down. Three points of contact at all times.* We knew these words well, and our feet found the old hollows; our hands used the strength of rainforest roots to pull us higher. Sometimes, a bull ant crawled over our fingers, and we held steady, watching it pass over the ridges of our knuckles. A huge carpet python lives in these cliffs, and we often saw her curled between two trees on the only path that led upward. Our faces passed hers as we climbed, so close that we could see the diamond patterns of her skin. This first climb leads to *The Gap*, an indent between the mountains that feels like the edge of everything. It was our halfway point, and we nestled between the carved stones and wild orchids, the elation of the climb already holding us in its grip. We rested, perched on the edge, watching the valley beyond.

ANASTASIA: *One of my earliest memories is being carried along this path. As a toddler, I sat on my dad's shoulders and touched the spiky vines and wet mosses as we climbed. I found my way across streams and was passed up cliff faces, watching as my family scrambled up to me.*

At twelve, I remember leading the group. With the hidden path ingrained in me, I would run ahead, navigating the rainforest. Reaching the massive strangler fig, I turned toward the cliffs, following the afternoon light to the west. I looked back through the palm trees, my long shadow reaching past the rocks. Watching my family follow my chosen path, I understood these mountains as my home.

From *The Gap*, we used the vines to ascend rocky cliffs, and suddenly the forest changed from thick bush to grassland. We followed the ridgeline, grass towering over us and snakes slithering past quicker than we could see. There was one last horizontal climb, and as we pulled our bodies up over the highest rocks, the view opened around us—we could see all the way to the ocean. Our eyes traced the dense bush we had passed through, the speckled banana plantations and the winding valley to the farm—a tiny patch almost engulfed in the mountain's shadow. The volcano caldera is obvious from here, a huge crater surrounding us.

JULIA: *The last time I climbed the mountain was in spring. We reached the top and watched the light fade from the valley. Between the two big boulders that sit on the cliff's edge, we found a spot with the best views of the night sky. We set up our camp, collecting sheafs of grass as our beds. On the edge of the cliff, we lit a campfire, a circle of our friends' faces illuminated like the last light on the mountains. We shared mulled wine and stew that we managed to haul up on our backs. Each friend that joined us on this adventure became family. They laughed with our parents and brother and uncles; our whole world was gathered together, and on this last climb, we celebrated my final days before leaving for the city.*

When everyone was asleep, I lay awake with my eyes on the stars. They were closer than ever before, some shooting through the night sky, some hanging suspended like beacons. In that bed of grasses high above the world, sleeping was different. I remained conscious of all the movement around me: aware of the moon's path, its light glistening off gum leaves throughout the night. The snakes and beetles were silent, but I could feel their presence in the trees. The tilt of the stars encircled my sleep. I felt Earth on its axis, the coming of dawn like a wave. I woke with an understanding of my duty to this rainforest that raised me. Everything I knew was within this caldera, the patterns of my life carved by these ridges.

The sun rose over the ocean, gold-reflecting water spreading like ink. It slowly illuminated the valley from which we grew, the mountain whose wisdom guided us to become the women we are today. The seasons still circle around the mountain's peak and tell us that for every lesson we learn, we are indebted to these lands and waters.

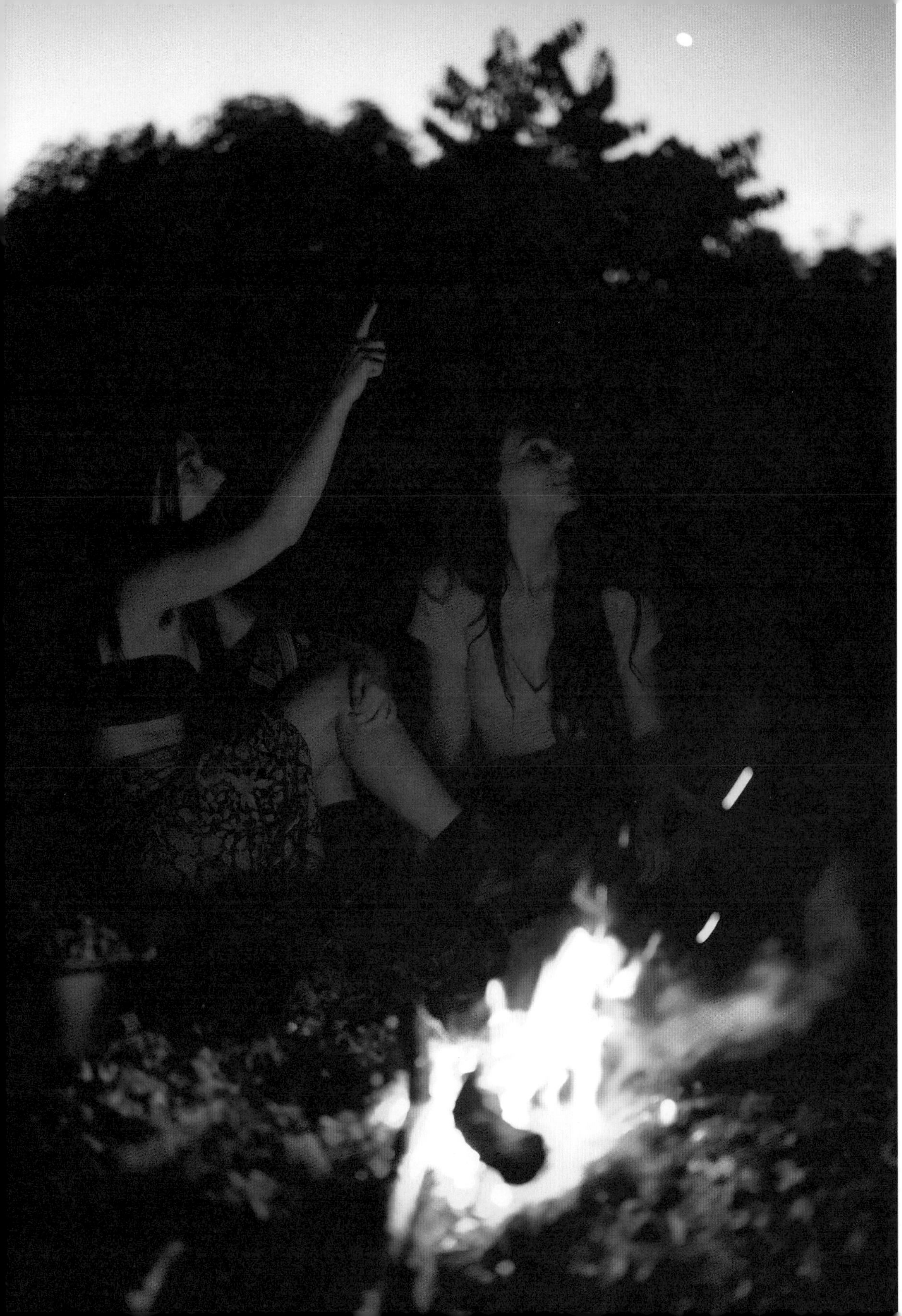

THE RETURN

The first thing we noticed was the mountain. Blue shadows stretching, it stood like our mother above us, unchanged. We traced the map of its horizon without thinking, our fingers following her curved peak, down the ridgeline of jagged rainforest to *The Gap*. Through *The Gap* is where storms come; you look toward its shape in the afternoon, and a darkened, bruised sky tells you that rain is coming.

But no rain clouded *The Gap* on that afternoon of rebirth. It was the first day of spring and our dad had just died. We returned home into the shadow of the mountains with new eyes. We looked to the west, and in the silhouetted peak we saw him there, just beyond the rays of spring's hazed shadows. In our shock and grief, the landscape held us. We found our mum and our rainforest home the same as they always were, but a weight had shifted within us all. Still, the light slanted through the windows, the veranda step warmed in the afternoon sun, and the streams trickled from the mountains above. The chickens scratched at our feet as we threw them grain and collected their eggs. The sheep were on the highest hill, still waiting for our dad to come and shepherd them as he always had.

Walking up the ridge, we followed the curve of the landscape. The path was worn and familiar at our feet. At the top of the hill there is a view of the whole valley; each mountain acts as a direction on our internal compass. To the west is *Mother the Mountain*. South are the fatherly cliff faces. East is the faint blue line of the ocean. North are the mountains that we call *Skyline*. From here, the whole farm

looked immense: the rainforest was intertwined with patches of orchards, and the lake reflected the fading light above. We saw each tree, each animal, and stream as a detail in our story, a fleck of significance, reminding us of our responsibility. This weight shadowed us as the sun began to fade.

A black cockatoo's song filled the sky. It encircled us, twirling through the clouds. The long grass rippled with the wind. The tiny fruit trees at the bottom of the valley were softly blanketed in the spreading dark. The wind blew through us, and we walked along the ridge line. Our fingers brushed against each plant with unconscious knowledge. Without thought, we knew every grass by its smell, its touch, the noise of its seeds shaking to the earth. Their roles were mapped in our minds as clearly as the mountains around us. The threads that connected each plant reached through the soles of our feet and brushed at our fingertips. As we walked, we were pulling weeds without thinking, instinctively collecting and spreading the seeds of those that belong.

We called the sheep home and waited, thinking of our dad who climbed this same mountain and waited for these same sheep. Imitating his herding call, we contorted our voices to morph into his deep, loud *c'mooon*. In return, we heard a faint *baa* from Uno, the leader of the flock. She was the first sheep ever born on the farm, and by our side, she grew from a tiny, playful lamb into the matriarch of the herd.

That day, sweet Uno sang back to us with her deep, gentle *baa*, and soon each sheep came running through the trees, bouncing over cliffs and winding through vines and

bush. The shadows shifted in the mountains as they always had. The sheep came running like they always did. Our dad was gone, but his herding call still echoed through these hills.

The sheep followed us back down, through the forest, fruit trees, and tangled bush. We touched each trunk and vine as we passed. Our place, and our role within them, was immense and tiny all at once. In the reverie of their grasp we understood what it means to live with nature, to know our place within its web. The path before us was clear. The soil and birds and plants and trees were holding us as one with them.

That afternoon was the beginning of an immense journey: a return of surrender unto ourselves and the land. It was a passage through hardship that would teach us everything. We found ourselves as three women—our mum and us—living in the rainforest alone. In each struggle we birthed a new version of ourselves, stronger with every simple thing we learned to do anew. We began to live with the cycles of this place, harvesting our own water and collecting our electricity from the sun. The food

that fed us grew from a seed to a vegetable in our hands. Seasons guided us, and we became the landscape. In this connection, we healed.

When the rains returned at the end of that long spring, we faced another reckoning. Uno the sheep, the matriarch of the flock, died of old age. But we watched the flock recover and continue to roam through the orchards. We saw her daughter, Aphrodite, take over as the leader. We began to see how much death is a part of the cycles of life. Uno went back to the earth, just as those before us have done. She lives on in her children, the fruit trees, and the grasses that grow. In the cycle of the flock, we understood our life on this earth not as a linear journey, but a circular movement. A moment in time, significant in its insignificance. Like a singular flower in our garden, growing and dying, feeding the earth as it rots, spreading seeds as it dries. We continued to shepherd through the hills, and everything made sense. The cycles of death and rebirth were as simple as Aphrodite's round eyes staring into our own, mirroring her mother.

60 YEARS OF RESTORATION

Sixty years ago, our grandparents came to this patch of earth under the mountain and began sowing seeds of care into the soft ground. They planted thousands of trees, spending their lifetimes with their hands in the soil—germinating seeds, planting saplings, and nurturing their growth into an immense forest. Through the wet gullies, they planted native rainforest trees while the steep hills were sown with the subtropical plants of the forest. Logged hillsides and bare earth transformed with life. As the roots of their plantings deepened, our grandparents grew old with the trees and became one with the earth.

Now, sandpaper figs, quandongs, and black beans form a thick canopy above us as we walk in wonder through these soft, ferny gullies. Macadamias, native plums, and towering gums fill the ridges, and between them grows every tropical fruit tree you could imagine. These valleys are covered with orchards planted by those before us, dotted with the fruits of their lives.

The best mango tree is up on the ridge, surrounded by the forest. Each summer its fruit is beaded throughout its massive branches. Our dad told stories of this tree, of him and his brothers climbing up high to reach the largest fruit.

Each year, the fruit returns, and each year we follow the leaning branches up into its arms. The climb is like a well-rehearsed dance, its movements are ingrained within us. Left foot interlocked in a hollow, right arm jumping to reach a smaller branch, sway three times, and with enough momentum, you can pull yourself up to the higher limbs. Climbing further and further, we get to the tallest branch. From here you can see the whole valley, the endless fruit

trees spread out across the land. Each tree is etched with the stories of those before. Memories connected by ripening fruit and vast orchards.

On the first summer after our return, the mangoes fruited with abundance. Their bright blooms had set in the dry spring, slowly forming fruit born of the flowers pollinated in our dad's care. In his absence, the fruit still grew, blossoming to nature's ever-continuing cycles of growth. Up high in the old mango tree, surrounded by this eternal fruit, we learned the meaning of stewardship. We looked out over the endless green and saw that planting a tree—this small action of your hands placing a sapling in the ground—can change a landscape. It can feed generations of people to come and provide shade and nourishment for endless life. More than this though, we began to grasp what it means to be stewards of the land. To honor the earth, to feel no ownership—only respect and reverence. To dedicate ourselves to tending a patch of ground.

We passed handfuls of golden, sappy fruit down to our mum, who waited at the bottom of the tree with baskets, a pair of pruning shears, and knowing in her eyes. She has carried the care of this land within her for years now. At the base of the tree, a cassia grew. Its bright yellow flowers fill the rainforest with their glow, but in their beauty is a hidden threat. They are an invasive weed that hinders the growth of anything around them. The pruning shears in our mum's basket were once our grandparents', and then our parents'. Their metal is smoothed by 60 years of hardened hands working with the curve of their handle, snipping weeds and pruning trees, nurturing endless growth. On that summer afternoon, our mum showed us how to use their blades to snip cassia at the base of its stem, allowing the mango tree to keep thriving for generations to come.

Under the old tree, we saw ourselves as a link in this chain of continued care. Our responsibility to the land became a tender gift. With mangoes in our hands and our mother by our side, we entered into the story of stewardship.

THE SECRET OF GIVING

The day before our dad died, he came home from the neighbor's house with a box full of ducklings. They were not yet a day old, and blinked and screamed of life. The mother duck had hatched a gigantic brood, too many to survive the eagles and carpet pythons. So our dad—the rainforest boy who always had ducks—spent his last day collecting this final gift for us. His whole life was spent living with the land, caring for his community, the earth, and the animals. With this cardboard box of ducklings, he showed us a path forward, a way to continue this cycle of giving.

We held and cared for the ducklings, and through all our struggles, they sang notes of joy into our lives. But they did something more than this. As we sat with them in the garden, we observed their first swims, and their discoveries of flowers and the warmth of the sun in the mint patch that lulled them to sleep. And then, we saw how they instinctively interacted within the web of nature. They began chasing grasshoppers and rummaging through the nasturtiums to find pests under the drooping leaves. Their tiny beaks nuzzled into the earth, aerating the soil, and behind them, in a trail of droppings, the garden grew like magic. With the help of ducklings, our world was fertile once again. They grew to become our companions and helped us care for the land. In this gift our dad left us, we learned to always give more than we take. This perspective changed our lives.

Suddenly, we saw this reciprocity all around us. As the sheep wandered the orchards, they ate weeds and fallen fruit, leaving their droppings at the roots of the trees as tiny gifts of fertility. These droppings would feed the soil and the trees to become next year's rich fruit in the sheep's mouths. The cycle of giving continued endlessly. The way we rotated the sheep's paddock each day let them move like a herd, mimicking nature. And miraculously, this movement allowed them to stay naturally free of worms and parasites. Something even more incredible was happening though: the land was responding to the sheep's care. As they grazed, a natural balance returned. A thick topsoil formed, and native grasses established themselves once again. We continued shepherding them from paddock to paddock, allowing the pasture to rest as the herd moved on. The grasses grew bright, with broad blades that absorbed so much energy from the sun to be passed on to the sheep and the land. As they ate, the sheep promoted even more growth. A beautiful, complex system was forming.

Following the guidance of the ducklings' gifts, we got two small goats. The sweet, bouncy sisters joined the team of rainforest restoration and began their work instantly. They started munching on the invasive weeds that the sheep weren't interested in. The camphor laurels and lantana began to wane, and in their place, beautiful forests of native hoop pines and tree ferns returned.

Like the magic of the ducks in the garden and the sheep in the orchards, we realized that we too can be a part of this graced interconnection of nature. We began small, clearing patches of invasive weeds and planting mulberries beside an old avocado tree. As we walked through the forests, those two little goats followed at our feet. We pulled clumps of lantana that took the strength of our

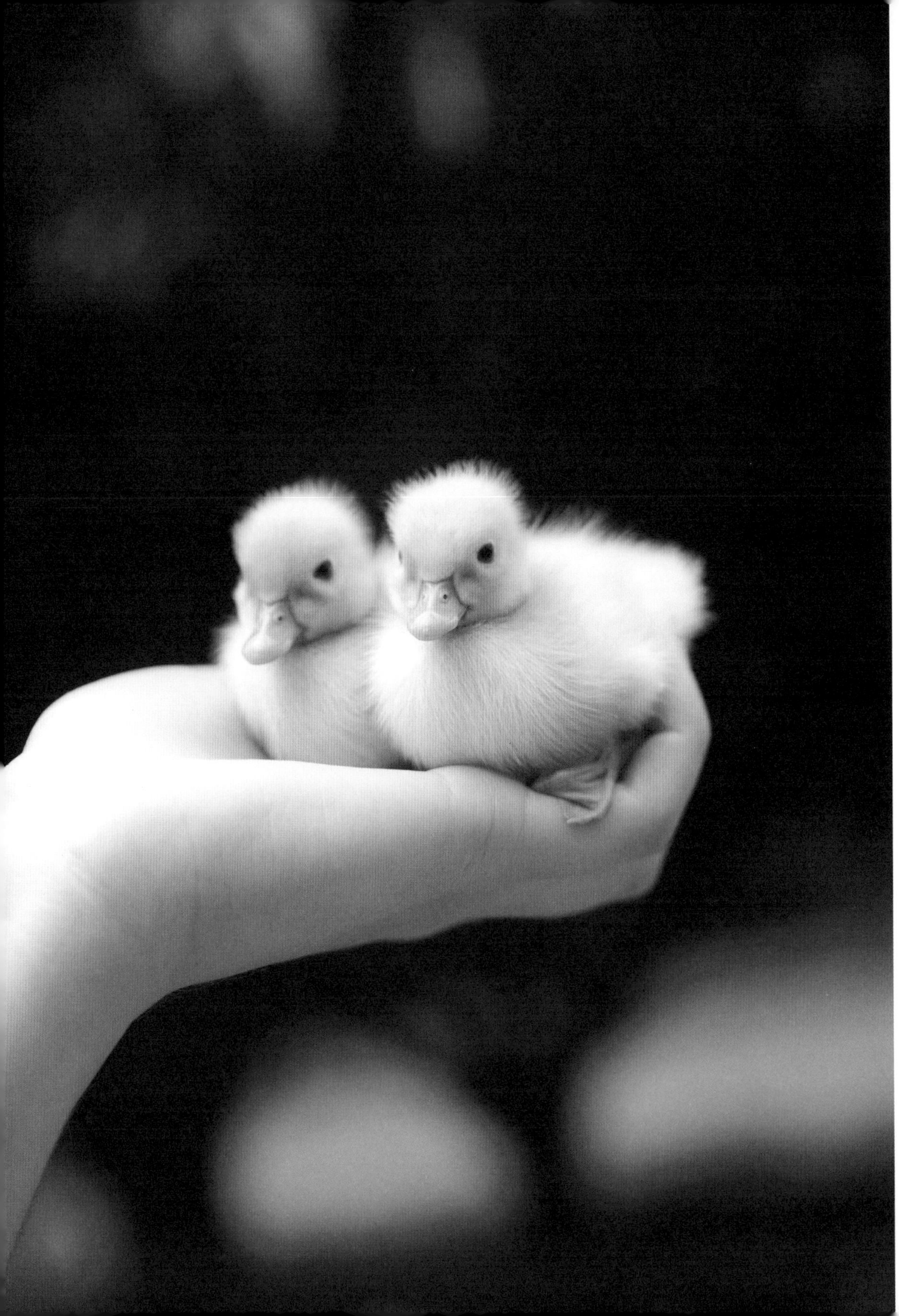

entire bodies to wrench their sturdy root systems from the
ground, and by our side, the goats munched on the fresh
leaves and green shoots, stopping the regrowth of this
all-consuming weed. The land began transforming in our
care. We planted orchards, fencing them off so that the
young trees would grow out of the sheep's reach. The ducks
foraged at the saplings' roots, keeping the grass down and
pests at bay. We planted native bunya pines, coolamons,
bangalow palms, and plums. And suddenly, we felt our
lives and energy woven into the land, connected in an
inexplicable way. The unwritten rule of reciprocity bound
us as one with the forest and bees, the grasses and trees.
This is the gift that our dad gave to us on his last day: the
ability to connect with the earth and her systems. To enter
into a relationship with the land, always giving more than
we take.

In autumn's soft sun, we hiked up the highest hill,
carrying a small sapling in our hands. The avocado tree
sown by our parents had started to flourish. They
planted it years ago, and from a small seed, it grew slowly
to become a strong tree with branches engulfed in fruit.
Above it, our grandparents' tree stood tall. Twisting
through the fading light, its bark was one with the
landscape. Carefully, we chose a spot just down the hill
and planted one of our own. We wove the sapling's roots
into the soil and felt ourselves stretch deep into the
ground with them. The afternoon left the sky empty,
and soon autumn's biggest moon rose to the east, gently
caressing the pastel hills. Moonlit beams reached
through the mist, like threads connecting everything.

THE FIRE

The fire came from the mountain. Burning from the west, it crawled slowly over all things that held meaning. First, our camping spot on the mountain's peak. Then, it followed the ridgeline that splits the valley in two, down toward our home—burning the old, hollowed bloodwoods, crossing banana roads and fire breaks.

We watched it for days; columns of smoke rising as the fire approached our home. It moved with a slow surety, the winds were on its side. It advanced unfalteringly through pockets of rainforest, burning places that had never been touched by fire before. The flames moved up the sides of ancient tree ferns, dislodging rocks that were held by vines, causing them to fall, tumbling into deep gullies. These falling boulders took coals with them, igniting rainforest valleys and spreading the fire's reach. Through palms and ferns it moved onward, unfazed.

In the time that our family has cared for this land, it has never seen fire like this. The mountains catch immense rains, channeling the water's abundance into the rich, volcanic soils to create delicate ecosystems of intense growth and vast biodiversity. This rainforest has been cared for by the Arakwal and Minjungbal People for more than twenty thousand years. Its history is held in the trees and waters and the people whose story it is to tell. But with colonization came so much ongoing injustice, dispossession, and loss. The great red cedars of these valleys were cleared and felled for their rich wood. Invasive species were introduced, choking the landscape with their ceaseless growth. A changing climate dried

pockets of wet rainforest to become fuel to fires that were once inconceivable in this place. The rainforest weeps, and in each burning ecosystem and lost story, we weep too.

From the front veranda of our home, we watched as the first flickering flames crept over the top of the hill. In our upturned faces, hazy in the light of that pink setting sun, we held four seasons of grief in our smoke-scratched eyes. A year had passed since our dad died, and on this anniversary, we stood together, facing a fire on the horizon of our world.

We couldn't sleep due to the smoke and the sounds of once great trees crashing down toward the gullies. In darkness, we hiked up the steep ridge to check how far the fire had come. As we walked up the path, the flames were close, edging their way down the hill toward us. The insides of old familiar trees were hot eyes of coals, and the tree ferns were engulfed. The fire was now a half ring circling us to the west. It had taken the old gums and the big bloodwoods where the black cockatoos sleep. We looked up to see the trunks of the oldest mango trees smoldering, the ones that our opa had planted. Their limbs that once felt like home were now blanketed in smoke.

From here, we looked out across the farm, the soft curve of the ridges were dark against the red night sky, with the sleeping valleys, orchards, and sheep still below us. Our dad was a firefighter; he knew every inch of these hills, just like we do. But in his care, the land never burned like this. In the year of his absence, we had learned to care for ourselves, the animals, and the land—to adapt with

Our brother, Riley, near the old mango trees at the top of the farm as the fire front approached.

the seasons, loss, and life. With the grand trees burning beside us, the path forward was hazed in smoke. But, we knew our duty was to care for these hills that hold us, so with the heat of the fire behind us, we shifted our shoulders, adjusting that weight.

Picking up our tools, we made firebreaks by clearing the ground of bush and leaf litter, creating a barrier to stop the fire's spread. We worked into the dawn to protect the old trees. The sun rose, and our community joined us. Every firefighter in the valley stood by our side. We cleaned the leaves from the gutters and cleared the bushes from around the shed and our house. We set up pumps and sprayed roofs down with water, clogging the gutters and letting them fill. Helicopters passed close by overhead. We watched anxiously as they filled their buckets from the lake and rose over the familiar ridges to the fire front, bombing the hottest flames with precious water. One bucketload landed near our brother—he is a firefighter like our dad was, and he joined his crew up in the tree line as

they tried to stop the fire. Up in the burning forest, he felt the spray of the helicopter's water. His uniform dripped in that hot, dry bush.

In the house, we packed the photo albums into boxes, stacking them in the center of the kitchen floor. We could feel the energy of the fire above us. It vibrated. But just as the flames were about to consume it all, the wind changed and the fire moved in a different direction.

We were lucky, but we grieved for the forest and the animals that were lost. These fires burnt with an unknown intensity. They were unpredictable, the seasons were different, and the weather was hotter and drier than ever before. The biodiversity lost in the heat of that fire changed us. We mourned for the rainforest and saw with immense clarity the need to protect nature and restore her balance. Making a vow to the earth, we promised to plant thousands of trees, to care for all creatures, nurture diverse ecosystems, and regenerate the land.

Seeds
of Change

A thousand ancient hands
are held within a seed's intention.
Our own hands twirl to their essence,
guided by the continuation of being.
Sprouts reaching through soft soil,
like silent echoes pressing through time.
Interlaced movements of the past and future
teach us the eternal dance of spreading seeds.

BEYOND SUSTAINABILITY

When the first rains fell after the fire, we felt the celebration of the earth beneath us. The dry soil blossomed into life once again. In an instant, every leaf opened in a blinding green light. The smell of petrichor—rain on earth—enlivened us too, and we danced in the rich humidity. Rainbows and mist filled every valley with triumph.

Years on, the earth still hurts. We can still see the touch of the droughts and fires on the land. The trees are scarred with burns blackening their trunks, and the old gums on the tops of the ridges who were starved of water stand dead, like ghostly reminders of our mistakes. But each day as we work to regenerate the rainforest, we feel the hope of a better future rising within us. With each tree planted and ecosystem nurtured, we sense a tide turning. With our help, the landscape is returning to health.

Down by the water, we see it all clearly. This is a place where our work is starting to show: rainforest trees grow tall and a sea of hoop pines are returning. Young coolamons are thriving, and native bees dance from lillypilly to lotus. Baby green tree frogs nestle in the curls of native grasses. This is where we come to sit and witness the return of balance.

A butcher bird sings above us and prompts us onward. He has lived alongside us for years. As we do regenerative work, he follows, knowing that when we pull weeds, we expose a rich underworld of grubs and worms that he can swoop in to collect. We walk up the valley toward the waterfall, and as we go, lantana bushes come easily from the wet, alluvial soil. This track is part of a wildlife corridor we created, which allows the passage of koalas, wallabies, and goannas from the mountains to the sea. Deep in this ferny gully, it feels as if we are in a secret passageway to another world.

The bangalow palms, black beans, blue quandongs, and sandpaper figs have dropped their seeds, and they lay scattered on the forest floor like shining gifts. We collect them in our palms, gently. These pearls of fertility lead the way to a regenerative future. The butcher bird watches from a fence post, and as we walk further into the dense bush, we pause and softly place these seeds into the earth. Sometimes we find a little hollow, a perfect place for a tree to grow; sometimes we pull an invasive weed, and in the disturbed earth left by its roots, we nestle a tiny seed. Soon we are deep in the gully with towering tree ferns above us and the waterfall trickling down. A family of kookaburras rest in the flooded gum tree, and their laughter echoes throughout the valley. We know each of them and remember when the youngest was just a baby learning to sing.

Here, the edges of the gully are either steep rock faces or slippery soil. In the heat of summer, we finished fencing this wild terrain. Determined and inspired, we set out to create a wildlife corridor and a fenced area to enable the goats and sheep to graze and help to restore the forest. It was one of our biggest and longest projects yet. Our whole community came together to help; our uncle taught us how to fence, dig holes, and ram poles into the gravelly earth. Our neighbor carried whole rolls of wire up on his shoulders, and together, we achieved what we thought

would be impossible. We fenced the wildest and roughest patch of bush, a place where it has always been too steep to hike.

Now, walking up and witnessing the change that the sheep and goats have made to this landscape—the clumps of invasive lantana, cow cane, and camphor laurels diminishing—fills us with the energy of the forest. The fire burned through here, but life is subtly returning. Nature is hungry to find balance, and when tiny inputs like the sheep's care, seeds scattered, or weeds pulled gather momentum, they begin a chain of growth. Nudged in the right direction, nature is finding her way back to health.

Deep in this valley are the twin red cedars. Like parents, their trunks connect at the base to form one. Together, their strong buttressed roots allow them to reach high into the rainforest canopy. Below them, we notice a whole forest of shooting saplings. A grove is filled with these babies that will one day grow to be grand trees: majestic giants that will fill the rainforest once again with their beauty. We sit among them and notice tiny sheep pellets at our feet. It is all connected.

Black cockatoos twirl overhead as they return home to sleep in the old, hollowed trees. Their great wingspan twists and glides between branches. They nestle their young here, up high in the safety of the forest. We view this valley as a little pinpoint of change. The black cockatoos' songs tell us that the future can be shifted through simple acts of nurture. If we apply this understanding to all aspects of our life, the potential of immense change appears before us. This is regenerative living: a way of being that steps beyond sustainability, always giving more than we take. It is knowing ourselves as an integral part of nature, seeing the trees and animals as kin, and understanding that each of our actions is woven within this interconnection. It is living as if the seeds of the future are at our feet, guiding our path toward a regenerative world.

GARDENING WITH THE EARTH

Our journey began with a simple dream: to live in harmony with nature. We wanted to grow our own food, to be self-sufficient, and to know our impact on the earth as positive. Seeking to give more and take less, we set out to live not just in nature, but with the earth. The ways of this regenerative life are told in the fabric of the forest. We looked to the wisdom of its weave and saw the answers of how to live with nature.

We started by building a garden from a patch of weedy earth. Lantana covered the hillside in a thick tangle that blocked the sun. We pulled it out by hand, with the goats by our side. Then, we didn't know what to do next. We'd watched our mum sow seeds and grow herbs and vegetables, but her ways seemed like magic to us. So, we started small and planted a patch of zinnias. They grew from the earth, their bright petals twisting toward the sun. But soon, the insects attacked, the mildew appeared, and the caterpillars crawled up their fragile stalks. In our ignorance, we had planted just one species, simplifying nature's diverse complexity. In this imbalance, weeds and pests grew, claiming the bare soil and lack of biodiversity. We couldn't restrain the powerful and unpredictable elements of nature, but we learned to honor this wildness, to revere nature's ability to reorganize herself from homogenous simplicity to tangled abundance.

We looked to the forest where an orchid grew between the old branches of a rainforest tree. The limbs were covered in mosses and the ground was thick with wild violet and ferns. Pollinators flew between the tunnels of trees. In the complex beauty of nature's systems, we saw an answer. We saw that the mosses and ground cover provided moisture, the orchids brought pollinators, and the trees' deep roots brought nutrients from below. Every plant was connected to the thousands around it. Instead of working against the innate intricacies of nature, we decided to work with them.

We returned to the garden with our pockets full of seeds, and planted marigolds that deterred the grasshoppers, alyssum that covered the ground and retained moisture, sunflowers that made huge stalks for the tomatoes to grow up, comfrey thats deep roots brought nutrients up from below, beans that fixed nitrogen, and African blue basil that attracted bees. The garden came alive with color, depth, shape, and texture, every plant unique in its beauty and purpose. We watched the pollinators return, the flowers grow tall, and the veggies flourish.

As always, the butcher bird watched us from his fence post. He would swoop down, collecting a grasshopper in his beak. From him, we learned that a garden reaches further than its plants; it extends outward into the environment and deep into the earth. So, we created a synthesis of systems: animals and plants all working as one. The ducks ate bugs at our feet just as the butcher bird did, mimicking the artful complexities of nature.

Then we looked further to the wisdom of the forest floor and realized that in nature, there is no bare earth: only mulch and growth, animals and trees. We learned to

never dig and expose the soil but rather to work with the animals to gently nurture its life—holding carbon and microbes in its richness. A team of chickens joined us. They instinctively turn mulch like their jungle bird ancestors, scratching to mix leaf matter, their own manure, and the earth to create rich humus perfect for planting straight into. Inspired by the forest, we mulched our garden heavily and planted trees and shrubs among the plants and ground cover. Some roots grew deep while some grew shallow; some plants provided shade while some brought nutrients. Others suppressed weeds and attracted insects. But together, they all grew abundantly. And like a forest, grassland, or any ecosystem, we planted

many varieties: a cosmology of species that thrived together in the wet soil and hot sun.

In the practice of gardening, we were suddenly linked to the source of our food, the seasons as they came and went, and nature's systems. We found the answers of how to live with nature hidden in the earth. The plants' simple truths were revealed to us in the many hours we spent with our hands in the soil, looking to the forest for guidance. They taught us that to garden is to dance with the earth; it is to follow the seasons, to trace the bees, to inspect the soil, and to work with the weather. It is to feel the connections around you and know yourself as an extension of this. It is to live in harmony with nature.

COLLECTIVE CARE

The old apricot tree grows on the lake's edge. It leans over the water with its twisting branches. Woven around the tree's timeworn trunk is a passion fruit vine that reaches with tendrils twirling between fruit and shimmering leaves. We float on our backs below this tree as the lake's reflections dance in the afternoon light. In the stillness, we float between scattered passion fruit dropped from the enchanted vine like treasured gifts bobbing between lily pads. They taste nothing like normal passion fruit: their flavor is deep and intense, an incomparable sweetness. But there was a time when we almost lost their riches, and as we float below—cracking thick purple skin to reveal dripping seeds and gold juices—we are reminded of this lesson. We savor their taste, and with the final seeds tenderly cupped in our hands, we swim to the bank and carefully wrap them in paper, saving them for the future.

This loving practice of saving seeds was taught to us in the droughts and fires when the passion fruit vine wilted under the relentless sun and collapsed into the last receding waters. We thought we had lost it forever. Remembering its magical fruit, we could almost hear the stories of the long line of seed bearers that had held its life in their care. Only then—in the passion fruit vine's absence—did we understand the importance of a seed. The vine had grown to become perfectly acclimatized to this rainforest's hot sun and heavy rains. These glowing seeds were resistant to pests and selected for their deep flavors. They had been sown and collected, passed between ancestors and savored by generations. But in our care, the

seeds had withered. We had broken the sacred chain of continuous giving.

With deep sadness we shared stories of the passion fruit's taste of pure gold, its curling leaves, its enchanting flowers, and its twisting tendrils. Through the community, these stories spread like seeds, and one day an old friend, who lives high in the rainforest, came to us with her arms filled with passion fruit. She had spent each summer floating in these waters too, grateful for the vine's golden gifts. What she said next changed our lives. She told us that a seed means nothing if you do not pass it on; a story is forgotten if you do not tell it. She told us that each time she eats a gift like these passion fruit, she saves the final seeds, treasuring them and holding them in her care.

When she passed these seeds back into our hands, we understood our duty to the future. We germinated them, and like summer's mist, they twisted and grew from the earth. Planting one below the apricot tree, we watched it intertwine itself once again with the old trunk. One seedling we returned to our friend up the valley, who had taught us what it means to give. The rest we spread like stories, passed between neighbors and friends with whispers of its sweet juices. Seeds exchanged between hands, and we saw this vine grow everywhere. In its abundance, we saw the culmination of endless generations of collective care. We saw the immense possibility of what humans are capable of. Together, we can share our seeds, our hardships, and our strengths.

Now, a nest of native bees has settled in the trunk of the old apricot tree. They fly from apricot blossom to

passion fruit flower, pollinating while collecting nectar
for the hive. In this tracing movement of light, they teach
us that to give is to receive. The act of giving is
instinctual and sacred: neighbors sharing seeds between
hands, the way a bee pollinates a flower or an animal
intuitively cares for the land.

From this lesson, we became aware of a rift in the
continuous cycles of giving. Seed varieties are being
forgotten, bees are going extinct, and animal habitats are
being destroyed. This loss isn't owed to individuals; it is
the responsibility of corporations attempting to simplify
the deeply complex ways of nature. Single crops are grown
over vast landscapes, creating monocultures that take all
they can from the earth. They strip nutrients from the soil,
deplete water, and erase all biodiversity. The climate crisis
is fueled by this misunderstanding—that we can take from
nature and give nothing in return.

Sweet, generous bees trace these cycles of broken
reciprocity. When they pollinate a flower grown of
nonorganic seeds, they are often poisoned. They carry
the pesticide back to their hive, and a whole hive can
die from the touch of one pesticide-coated seed. We can
learn so much from these precious bees, whose crucial
existence is too often ignored in industrial agriculture's
destruction. They live with intentional and innate
reciprocity. Collaborating, they work as a community of
small beings creating big changes. Like a hive, we too
can live collectively for a regenerative future. By
growing food or supporting organic farmers, we can
protect bees, seeds, and our stories. We can work as
one, with our community, and with the earth, always
giving more than we take. This way of living is not new
or revolutionary; it is inherently human. Throughout
history, we have collectively safeguarded the seeds of
the future. In the hands of the people, the oldest, most
resilient varieties of plants and vegetables have been
protected for thousands of years. Our strength is in
our collective care.

THE FLOOD

There is a place in the fold between mountains, where all water meets. It cascades through bright blue pools, framed by palm trees and tall cliffs. The pools drip and fold into themselves: they are the air bubbles of ancient magma, and every time we bring someone new here, we whisper that no one knows how deep they reach. Suddenly they come to an edge, a huge cliff with water casting rainbows on the volcanic rock below. The water slips under us, over the edge, and from here, we can see the whole valley. This place is filled with memories: the patterns in the rock paint the seasons of our lives. We know the shape of each stone and the feeling of its curve in the soft water. Our own stories here only stretch as far back as our grandparents, but sitting at the edge, we imagine all the people who have gathered here for millennia, nurtured by the cool waters and the significance that they hold.

But one day, everything changed. The flood came fast and without warning. Over just one day and night, almost a meter of rain fell over this valley. The noise of that much water falling with such force was deafening. We cowered inside our home, terrified and waiting. We could hear the thud of boulders as they rolled down the ancient creek beds, dislodged by the strength of the water. Rising temperatures have made our storms bigger and more unpredictable; our summers have become wetter, and our winters drier. In the noise of the flood, it felt as if the earth herself was crying out for help.

We woke to find that the landscape had crumbled around us. Landslides ripped through the rainforest and across roads, swallowing some of our neighbors' houses in a wave of red, clay earth. The bridges were gone, and every road was cut across with water. We were trapped with no one to rely on but ourselves. We spent the first few days hiking through rubble, with landslides, craters, and sinkholes filling our path. There was no way to know who was safe, so we hiked to find our neighbors and family, collecting stories along the way. From friend to friend, we passed news of who was okay and what had been lost. And in a beautiful wave of unsaid giving, our whole community came together like family. We shared food and cared for one another without hesitation. Digging landslide debris away by hand, we cleared roads and moved boulders. Where bridges were washed away, we built pulley systems. Those on the other side sent food and medical supplies along these shaking wires. With only hand signals and the look in our eyes, we spoke across the raging river. The disaster stripped us to our core, but in all the loss, something remarkable happened: everyone gave all that they could.

The earth still held us. She, too, still gave her abundance, and we collected baskets of fruit to feed the community. Instead of fearing the environment that threatened us, we only found more connection.

When the sun returned, we gathered by the creek and stood in the wake of the flood. Surrounded by the women of these hills, we traced the path of the water's destruction. Carving cliffs into the earth, leaving trees uprooted, and rolling boulders the size of houses, it left nothing untouched. These streams that once held us

were unrecognizable, and we all felt the same way—we all grieved with the earth. Together, our weathered hands pointed. We started finding landmarks: a boulder that remained in place, the coolamon tree still standing strong. We found the remnants of all that we love. So we sat together with our neighbors and told stories of love to the earth. Like us, these women grew up here. They bathed their grandchildren in these same streams. We all spoke of our love of the waters, the way we knew each stone, pool, and pebble as well as our own skin. And in this connection, we found so much hope.

Through disaster, our stories were woven even deeper into the earth. The need to give and protect grew stronger within us. We didn't speak of fear, but rather about the power of collective action. Weaving stories around the beauty of the land, we spoke about how the care of our community was far stronger than the force of the storm. Together, we had all learned something immense. We were galvanized in the understanding that these events, although terrifying, prompted us into action. We learned that if we always hold within us a connection to the land and a willingness to care for it, we can face the climate crisis. We can give our skills as gifts to those around us. Like the coolamon tree, the animals, and the bees, we can exist in an endless cycle of giving and receiving. This might just be what saves us.

REGENERATIVE PRACTICES

Nature as Self

Return to nature, and see that you are not separate. The grand web of interconnection holds you among the trees, creatures, stars, and wind. Watch the perfect synchronicity of the earth's systems and know that these harmonies move through us all. United with the seasons, animals are kin, and you are one with the earth.

Be at Home

Return home into the cradling arms of the earth. To be at home in a landscape, you must contribute small gifts, as your energy is what makes you belong. Acts of care are what tie you to a place: like planting a seed or tree, noticing beauty, collecting little pieces of rubbish, or pulling a weed. Feel the earth beneath your feet, and inscribe your care in return. If you give even the smallest amount, you are connected. You are home.

Give More Than You Take

Return all that you are given. See nature's fluent circularity: a bee collects nectar for its hive and in return it pollinates the flower. Move toward this silent language of trust. Inhale the gifts of life: food, shelter, and care. Exhale unspoken reciprocity, returning nurture to the earth.

Co-responsibility

Return to a simple way of thinking: see the transience of life and the permanence of waste. Be responsible for each action. Act as if your own hands farmed the food you eat, sewed the clothes you wear, or mined the energy you consume. Live as if your hands will carry the weight of your waste eternally.

Collective Thinking

Return care to your community. Know that each gift is reciprocated: like the ocean's tides, there is always an ebb to the flow. Give joy, understanding, or just a passing smile, and see this optimism surge through the community. The ocean is built from many waves; there is power in the collective.

Grieve for the Earth

Return care to the earth that holds us. Feel deeply, sensing nature's wounds as our own. Grieve for the earth but not in despair. See that compassion is born from pain; let it compel us to find our role as protectors. Find hope woven through every element of life. Rebirth is as simple as a new moon pressed against the fading sky. See the seasons return, and understand nature's innate ability to heal.

Living with the Seasons

In spring she sprouts,
her growth rises to the unreachable sun.
In summer she grounds,
her roots move like the earth's gentle hands.
In autumn she blooms,
her petals permeate across her core.
In winter she wilts,
her seeds scatter in one last breath.
Their movement writes the future to the wind.

FINDING A NEW PATH

Our *Mother the Mountain* has always stood, cradling us in
her certainty. Each day, the sun sets behind her peak, her
shadow slowly stretching outward as she shields us in its
depth. But when the floods came, she crumbled. A
landslip tore away her mountainside, and the earth
collapsed into itself.

 The old path to the mountain's peak was lost, only a
bare, red cliff remained—stubborn and impassable. Each
grand tree that once guided our way had faltered and
fallen; the only sign of their existence was the tops of the
tallest palm trees scattered like matchsticks. The landscape
was swallowed in a sea of rubble.

 Months after the flood, we woke early and began to
traverse the mountain's base. The familiar path through
the banana plantations had slipped away into cliffs and
gorges, but we climbed up and through to the edge of the
rainforest once again. We set out to carve a new path.
Forcing our way through lawyer vines, we pushed
through the tangle of rainforest. Following only each
other's voices, we fumbled through dense bush so thick
we couldn't see through the vines and palm fronds. But
each track led to the same taunting rock faces and
rubble. We stood under the cliffs of clay, and they
reflected ominous red light onto everything we once
knew. There was no way forward. Staring into the eyes
of the climate disaster, we understood that as nature
crumbles, we do too.

 The creek still curled beside us, subtly winding
through the valley as it always has. The water pooled and
changed shape, cascaded, and emerged. Slowly, we began

to follow its organic path that was softly carved through the rainforest. The persistent trickle of water showed us the way forward. It was to live with nature's rhythm, flowing around each obstacle with her gentle tenacity. Climbing higher, we traced the ancient tree roots that held the creek's blue, shining waters. The afternoon sun stretched through an archway of trees, and a flock of black cockatoos glided above, following the sunlight as it spread. They landed in the old she-oak whose roots stretched knowingly, holding boulders in their grip. We followed the cockatoos' screeches as they feasted on its cones and dropped seeds into the smooth, glistening water below. The seeds swayed across ripples, starting their long journey downstream. Guided by nature's interconnection, we found a new path to the mountain's peak.

At the highest point, we watched over the vast rainforest, in awe of its grandeur. There were patches of bare earth, ravaged by the flood, but from here, we could see the rainforest returning. A delicate system of plants spread to cover the broken earth. Hopeful macaranga saplings grew from the cracks of destruction. Old roots of rainforest trees stretched over cliff faces. We saw the relationships that anchored each plant and animal into harmonic existence and understood ourselves as part of this.

The last golden rays of sun hit our faces and held us in their reach. We stood on the top of the mountain, and we saw that we are not separate from nature, but one with the grand systems of being, connected in synchrony. With new minds, we walked with the rhythm of nature down the mountain, following the continuity of the water's path.

ROUTINES
AND RHYTHMS

———

The seasons' voices speak answers; we follow their
cycles and learn from the earth's gentle ways. Great
shifting shadows spread across the mountains, and their
changing light acts as a calendar. The caldera's edge
cradles the valley like restful hands. Its cliff faces are our
clock: they stand still between the movement of time. In
summer, the mist curls between their crevasses. In
autumn, the shadows turn deep blue, leaking down the
stone like ink. In winter, the cliffs celebrate the start and
end of each day in a heavy, diffused pink. In spring, the
rock is dry and golden, waiting for the depths of the
wet summer's rains. The seasons paint the landscape
with their perpetual brush.

Summer

We follow the seeping summer light through the orchards and find the sheep under whichever tree is fruiting. They collect thousands of lychees in their mouths with a strange sheepish grin. Then, they hop and bounce away to the next fruit tree, so we follow quickly behind. In their collective memory, the sheep hold the most detailed map to the rambling orchards. They know every tree and in which season its fruit will ripen. We crawl on our knees through their intricate tracks, watching them bounce away across the horizon. Finally, we find them surrounding a jaboticaba tree, inhaling the sweet fruit straight off the trunk. From here, the easiest way home is to swim across the lake. We dive into the golden ripples, engulfed by the vast, cool waters.

Autumn

After summer's energetic rains and growth, we feel the pace slow in autumn. On these days, we calm with the seasons, following no routine but the flowing water and shifting sun. We celebrate the clarity that the softening weather brings. The creeks are full and opalescent; the skies shine golden sunbeams through the forest. Further up the valley, waterfalls flow over the cliffs. Our bare feet skip across river stones, and we find sparkling crystals uncovered in summer's floods. Under the palm trees, we play like children again. We camp in the rainforest and light fires under the stars. The constellations shine the brightest on these clear nights, and we count shooting stars through the glistening canopy.

Winter

The cliff face tells us that it is winter again when it sits pink and still. It is the season of sun as a soft light pours over everything. In the morning, it is cold, but as the sunlight falls on our bodies, we leave our jumpers behind. We follow the rising sun with goats following closely behind us. They bounce and hop around each corner, winter's dry grass cracking under their hooves. On top of the highest hill, there is a gate that leads to the dense forest. We let the goats through, and they skip off into the distance, quickly swallowed by vines and huge tree trunks. The grass is sparse in the dry season, so they love this wild paddock the most. It isn't fenced, so if they wanted to, they could run off over the mountain, but they never do. Each afternoon, we come back up the hill, and they are waiting for us by the gate, tired and full from a big day exploring. We walk them home and collect firewood under our arms. Through the depths of the rainforest, we walk fast since the air is chilled down here. In winter, the light never hits these pockets, and the ferns stand still and cold.

Spring

In late spring, the storms come and break the dry season in their resonance. As the year returns, so do the black cockatoos. Their arrival heralds the beginning of the monsoon; they bring the first rain on their wings. Wet drops hit the dry earth as they glide from valley to valley. We celebrate these gloomy days with our feet dancing in the muddy soil as the cockatoos circle above. Their laughter squeals in response to the sound of the storms, and we learn to sing out in joy with them, spinning in the significance of the first rain. The cockatoos teach us to glide along with the rhythm of the seasons, to tune ourselves to the cycles of the sun and moon, the wet and dry. These black cockatoos, the morning mist, the afternoon light, and the rising moon are all examples of the season's intricacies, serving as gentle reminders of the beauty of our world. They let us remember this forgotten way of being by connecting us to the earth and her seasons.

A YEAR OF SEASONAL EATING

When the first drops of spring's rain fall, everything bursts into life. Green and vibrant, the trees and plants and grasses grow with cavernous hunger. Jaboticabas fill out like shiny eggs on the trunks of the trees. Their insides taste like the riches of the wet season. If the rain comes at just the right moment, the mango and lychee flowers have already been pollinated and their fruit begins to grow. The jambu draw energy and water from summer storms, quickly filling into bright gems. They are watery apples that grow on trees, and on a hot day, their juicy insides are a glass of cool water growing in the middle of the forest. Plums, peaches, and pears fill the orchard with their fragrance.

The hot sun hits the moist soil, and the air is swimming with humidity. We wait for the wild summer storms to roll in through the mountain gap and cool the day. Mangoes, lychees, and longans burst into life. The fruit is filled by the rain, as the sun ripens their sweet flesh to create a taste that reminds us of summer's sunshine. The most amazing flavors are provided by nature with perfect timing; there is no better feeling than the end of a hot day, sitting in the shade of a mango tree and eating that sunshine flesh. With green mangoes we cook curries spiced with whatever grows in the summer: lemongrass, curry leaves, chilies, some ginger, and turmeric stored from the winter harvest. The mangoes often ripen quicker than we can eat them, so we preserve them into sauces and chutneys; freeze hundreds; sell them at the markets; or trade them with neighbors for sweet potatoes, rice, or coffee. The lychees and longans are precious gifts to take in your pocket on a hike or share the joy of their popping

insides with friends. Jambu continue fruiting throughout the summer, so we collect as many as we can, leaving some at the base of the tree for the sheep, insects, and the tree herself. We make jambu preserves that are the color of a pink sunset. Months later, when it is time to eat these ferments, we have almost forgotten the taste of their waxy flesh and the bountiful frenzy of summer.

Soon, the monsoon comes, the rain falls heavily for weeks, and our roads are cut by the raging streams. This time of year is always our reminder to slow down and let the seasons guide our routine. During these weeks, when we are trapped away from the world, the rain falls thick, and the mud reaches our knees. There is often no electricity and nothing to do but read or play board games, preserve food, and cook for each other. In this isolation, there is a kind of simple magic. To be at the mercy of the weather makes us remember nature's strength. It reminds us that we cannot change her to fit our needs, but instead we must adapt as the seasons do. We must echo the rain's steadiness with our own and feel the call of growth in the sun's energy. We know food as a precious resource and water as the bringer of life, gifting us nourishment and perspective.

The wet season is muddy and long, but nature guides us through this as well. She gives us lemon myrtle: a rainforest shrub that makes an antifungal tea. It tastes of lemons when we are months from the citrus season and the limes haven't ripened yet. When the rains subside and the creeks return to their paths, they slow into a shimmering flow. The air is clear and glowing, and the stars shine bright. This is the time when we are most busy;

the weeds grow furiously, and the fruit is abundant. Rested after the isolation of the wet season, we are ready.

Every few years, the bunya nuts fall. They are ten kilogram spiky cones that fall from the top of giant trees that have been here far longer than we have. The nuts are an important part of Indigenous culture and have been used as bush food for thousands of years. It is with great respect that we accept this gift from the bunya forests, always reflecting on the significance of the protein-filled seed that can feed hundreds of people. At summer's end the native plums drop their fruit. They are found only in this rainforest and their purple blue plums dot the forest floor—the same color as a late summer shadow.

As autumn comes, she brings macadamia nuts. They too are native to this rainforest and mature just as we need their protein for the dry season to come. The nuts are a precious resource that we store in big tins on the top of our pantry. We harvest jackfruit throughout this time as well, whether it is green or ripe. It is a quest to climb up the long, slippery trunk and pry the ten kilogram fruit from its stalk while avoiding spikes and sap stronger than glue. They fall to the ground with a thud, and we collect them with awe. It is a long walk home from here with this incredible fruit on our shoulders, spikes digging into our backs. Its riches will feed us for months. Then, the avocados ripen. From autumn to spring we celebrate their

creamy flesh—each perfect fruit feels like a miracle. The kiwis, carambolas, and finger limes ripen too, just when we need them. They fruit all the way into winter when we are craving vitamin C. The pecans drop when the days shorten, just before the citrus season that gives us oranges, lemons, and mandarins. Winter's custard apples ripen heavy on the tree.

Then comes the time when we harvest the green papayas, fermenting them with turmeric dug straight from the ground. In the middle of the dry spring, just like magic, the black sapotes ripen. We climb the tree and peel apart the heavy heart-shaped fruit to find its chocolate center. We take spoonfuls straight from the velvety insides, and it tastes like chocolate pudding—pure bliss from a tree. We make teas from cinnamon myrtle and African blue basil. Mulberries, strawberries, and raspberries fill our bellies and stain our hands. Then, the dry spring is broken and the wet summer returns. The season of frenzy begins again.

Some trees, plants, and vines endow us with gifts year-round. We can always rely on limes, bananas, and passion fruit. But it is the seasons that make these taste so special: the mulberries of the dry and the jaboticabas of the wet; winter's kiwis and autumn's jackfruit. The way they grow alongside the veggies and spices that complement their flavor—this rhythm is curated. We need no recipe book but the one that nature gives us.

A Year of Sustainable Eating

87

THE WATERS

Down by the water, there is a grand coolamon tree. Through the floods and fires, and each season's tide, this tree has stood steady. The rise and fall of the creek at its feet maps the movement of the seasons. It has witnessed the ongoing pulse of countless wet summers and dry winters.

This solemn tree is a remnant of the ancient rainforest that once spread from the mountains to the sea, but now, few of its kind remain. The coolamon's pink flowers are so rare that as they shower down, they cover the earth with lessons: a pink blanket of blossoms reminding us never to continue the mistakes of the past.

In the first seasons after we returned, we carried a fear of nature's force. We looked to the forest, and in the tangle of limbs, we only saw our responsibility. Hungry goannas clawed at our chickens, venomous snakes slithered on our front step, and pythons curled in the rafters above our beds. In our reliance on erratic rains for water, we felt the vulnerability of our existence. We knew each glass of water was a precious resource that would carry us through the dry season. But then, the rain fell, and in the chorus of heavy drops hitting the tin roof, we felt the rapture of our tanks filling with precious drips. The sun shone and heated the abundant waters of autumn, and we showered with a deep and joyous appreciation. When the trees fruited and vegetables grew from nothing but soil and seeds, water, and love—the feeling of feeding ourselves from this miraculous gift opened something within us. We uncovered a hidden part of ourselves that awakened in the wonder of each season and day, each creature and seed. We learned to tenderly wrangle the pythons as our dad once

did. Gently holding their thick, scaled bodies in our hands, we respected the strength of their presence and released them to sleep in a tree outside our window.

Now, we know that we can't live against the flow of the seasons. We swim and celebrate the water when the rains fall, and carefully collect it for when they don't. When food grows abundantly, we share, preserve, and feast. When it slows, we understand the significance of each bite. We don't live separately from nature, but gratefully within her.

On the water's edge, we spend our days planting coolamon saplings, imagining a time when their blossomed trunks are no longer rare, but encircle our water systems, their roots holding creek beds in place. It will be many years until they grow tall enough to shade this bank, but with our hands in the soil, we understand that this is how you learn to belong in a place, to sow gifts for the forest and for the future. In this action, we become a part of nature's systems.

The rewarding work of tending the land roots us into this earth. We stand under the coolamon tree and observe the stream spilling onward; each action we take pulsates outward through nature. Like tiny affirmations of our work, young green tree frogs breed around the coolamon saplings, and a baby red belly black snake sleeps on the hot rocks by the water's edge. We haven't seen its kind in years, and instead of fearing its deadly venom, we celebrate its return.

The creek flows on, making its way to the sea. It carries our actions with it; our lives are woven in the water's cycles. We cup this water in our hands and it sits smooth for a moment, reflecting our faces in a pure gaze. A rippling mirror of truth. It trickles through our fingers and continues its journey downstream. Once again, it will become the sea and the clouds, the rain, and the streams. Held in its grip, we understand that as the earth flourishes, we flourish too.

The Waters

EARTH PRACTICES

Celebrate the Sun and the Rain

Remember that the season's cycles are beyond our control. The rain fills the creeks and rivers; it nourishes the gardens, forests, and soil. The sun's light fosters the fruit trees and flowers to blossom. Nature teaches you to celebrate it all.

Walk Barefoot

Remember to let your feet touch the soil. The reaching grass can whisper the earth's secrets. Barefoot in the garden, you can feel the hollow of a rotten tree root or the damp mosses and leaf mulch. You can feel the compacted soil or the warmth of the compost. Your feet become rooted in the ground where stories and lessons vibrate beneath you.

Follow the Moon Cycles

Remember the world is magic at night. The fruit ripens to lunar phases, and saplings grow best when planted just past a full moon's shine. With an empty sky, the glow worms light up the forest while the moon's gravitational pull orchestrates the ocean's tide. Look up at the same moon that harmonizes nature, feel her light falling on your face, and know yourself as a part of this rhythm.

Wander Aimlessly

Remember to wander like a child again. Follow the afternoon sun deep into the twilight, or ponder the intricacies of nature's patterns. Feel the depth of your senses, and use them to find magic in everything: each star, leaf, or ripple.

Notice the Stars

Remember to watch the night sky. The simplicity of twinkling stars lets you realize the vastness of life and the beauty of your insignificance. As the constellations trace that sweeping movement over and over again, you can feel Earth's rotation. Witness the movement of the universe, and understand your place within it.

Connect to the World

Remember that you are always connected to the earth's cycles, which continually flow through our lives. Welcome nature inside with flowers on the table, a breeze that softly passes through the open door, or the tastes of seasonal food. See nature's eternal rhythms, and let them remind you to move with the earth.

PART II

CREATIVITY

"Living a life in tune with nature, creativity becomes the vessel through which we give to the world."

Language of the Hands

The dragonflies' wings flutter as our own hands do,
they weave meaning into everything they touch.
The falling leaves wander as our own minds do,
they dance to the rhythm of the wind.
The bees create as our own hearts do,
they fill their lives with beauty and purpose.
This meaning, this vision, this intention,
it is the art of living.

ART AS A WAY OF LIFE

In our slow life, we learn to view the world with awe. We hear poetry in birdsong and observe the dance of the moving seasons. With perspective, we perceive each moment as a curated composition painted by the earth. Honoring the gift of nature's beauty, we tell stories of love. We make paintings, write poems, cook, grow, sew, and dance. We give back to the earth that holds us. In each stroke of care, the love spreads. It heals.

In the garden, it is simple. We see beauty in every tiny thing. The cicada's song or the symmetrical petals, even a bug-eaten leaf with a spiral of small holes painted softly—it is all art. We cherish the harmonious disarray of gardening so that the act becomes a balance of beauty and practicality. We grow broccoli for the nourishment, but flowers for the joy. We celebrate color, placement, light, and dark. Big bushes of cosmos dance in the wind while small pansies frame the path. Hedges of African blue basil create shadows, and wispy dahlias grow tall above.

The tropical fruit trees celebrate a spectrum of each color: red Brazilian cherries, orange mangoes, yellow guavas, green papayas, blue native plums, purple grumichamas, and the iridescent pink of autumn's jambus. Looking to the fruit trees' vibrance, we cook with the same generosity held in their branches. With jambus, chilies, herbs, and spices in our baskets, we craft each element to become one, converging tastes, smells, textures, and spices. We nourish ourselves, family, and friends and instill gratitude for the earth into each bite.

Our life has become a collection of artful moments. Restoring the rainforest has started to feel like a dance.

As we plant a tree, our hands compress the soil around its tender roots in a rhythmic movement. We hold the future landscape in our minds as if we are composing a painting: we imagine a mulberry tree's long limbs will reach for the sky while a bunya pine's dark foliage will shadow this ridgeline for centuries to come. And it is as if the earth dances back. Rain showers down, watering the saplings with its prosperity. Sun reaches softly, fueling their growth with potent force.

As the last light highlights the hills, there is a sense of wonder in all that is around us. The mountains are tinted pink in the setting sun, and the world feels still, just for a second. The sounds of the rainforest encompass us: the kookaburras' laugh, the cicadas' song, and the frogs' chorus is deafening. With our feet in the wet earth, we look up to see a flock of white cockatoos sweep across the valley, screeching as they twist and drop into the forest.

A summer thunderstorm soaks our bodies in an instant and monsoonal raindrops fill the sky. Instead of being caught in routine, we have learned to dance in the freedom of the moment. We skip with joy, sing songs to the ducks, dress up in silly clothes, and dance in the rain. Even the most tedious jobs like caring for the animals become a daily expression of self: an embodiment of art. We learn from nature to make beauty in everything we do, honoring our inner selves by weaving the mundane with meaning. The art of life is found in the simplest moments.

We imitate the artful way that nature interacts in every element of our lives. Our hands dance across the garden, digging a hole for a seedling or collecting flowers for a vase. With joy, they plant trees, chop wood, fix fences, and build structures. In constant movement, our bodies become a brush for life's ever-evolving artwork. This is how we return the gifts of nature. We pause and notice, grateful for the setting sun and the feeling of the ground beneath our feet. We see the clouds, trees, and stars as an affirmation of our purpose: to sing these songs back to the earth.

PAINTING WITH NATURE
—by Julia

My studio windows frame the cliff faces' pink stone against the endless green of the rainforest. In each moment of clarity, I look above to their steadiness. Monolithic and unmoving, a constant flux of light falls across their stone. In stillness they reveal movement, and my brush follows this wavering stability, pulled by the motion of the sun. Always guiding, the cliff faces watch me too and the certainty of their balance guides my art practice.

In the cliffs' shadows, I see the strength of light. Before an empty canvas, I sketch compositions that reflect the harmonious relationship of human and landscape. In quick strokes, figures emerge from the canvas; the scene around them wrapping to the curve of their stance. Intuitively, I begin with the eyes. My brush moves in small, darting strokes, quickly filling color and depth, light and dark. Entranced, my face is just inches from the canvas as the gaze of my subject is slowly revealed, emerging outward from the center, spreading from the eyes. The fall of light on their face is like pink sun on rhyolite cliffs.

Still absorbed in the flow of the painting, I act without intention. My strokes drift onward to the background. Swirls of deep movement and fluid paint sweep like the sun and dancing leaves. Colors come to me like hidden messages. My palette is wild with wet paint, and I look above once more to the cliff faces, seeing beyond their surface of singularity to witness the myriad of hues that lie beneath their stone. I see that the sky is not one color, not one single blue, rather it shifts and changes each day, each moment, and each season.

Skin tones are green or orange or red or blue; shadows are purple; and clouds are not white, but every color you can imagine is painted within their luminance. Through color, I paint the complexity under the surface of each simple thing.

I take each moment step-by-step, absorbed in the details of every singular stroke, knowing its importance within the whole. Moving with a steady surety, I slowly carve a scene into the blank canvas. Then, I wake from the innate rhythm of painting. I step back and see the whole picture before me with a soft realization that this process is just like life. We must take each step at a time, letting our days be a collection of small, meaningful strokes rather than the pursuit of the whole. To paint is to learn how to become one with the unplanned currents of life.

This practice came to me when I needed it most. I was twelve years old and had just become chronically ill—a hardship that would shape my life from that moment on. Too sick to go to school, my mum brought home a big, empty canvas. I still remember the sight of it, leaning against the wall, filled with blank possibility. In that difficult time, I was gifted creativity.

Ravenous to learn, canvas upon canvas stacked up, filling the walls of our little rainforest house with bright scenes of women with long, wonky faces and staring eyes. I kept going, learning and growing. During those years, I must have made hundreds of paintings, and by the end, I could paint the most intricate eyes and hands to perfection. But I soon realized that it wasn't perfection I sought, it was the synthesis of meaning: a thousand small strokes becoming one. It was carving light into the darkness, finding beauty in the smallest moments, and accepting the process of life's journey. It was healing.

My art practice grew with me, and every moment of my life has been processed through paint. I traveled the world and learned to express my growth and wonder. Through the fires and floods, the grief and loss, I painted. Each day, I am drawn to document the landscape as it shifts with change, to storytell the seasons: the struggles and joy, and everything in between. My work always examines the inherent balance of things. The birth in death, the joy in sorrow, the light in darkness, and the darkness in light. I paint the relationship between humans and nature and how this bond changes as the environment shifts. Documenting the pain and hope of this pivotal time of environmental change drives me forward. I see the loose brushstrokes becoming whole, inscribing that deep connection and love for the earth, just as I feel grief over its destruction. In this, I face hardship and find hope within it.

Painting our connection to the landscape through each climate catastrophe and change reminds me of myself as a little girl—painting to heal, to tell stories, and to celebrate light in the darkness. I think that this is what it means to create: it is holding fearless hope in your heart in the face of anything.

REGENERATIVE SEWING
—*by Anastasia*

I've always been a sewer, ever since my mum first gave me a needle and thread as a tiny child and I turned our old tea towels into a wardrobe for my teddy bear. From that moment, I understood this is what I wanted to do: to create with my hands, stitching together each element of myself. My life revolved around this goal, and I moved across the country to study fashion. University gave me the skills to construct something from nothing. Like magic, creations from my imagination formed between my hands. I was inspired with new knowledge and techniques, but like unravelling seams, I noticed a disconnect in the fashion industry. Ethics and sustainability were overlooked for profit, and I sought to find solutions. After moving home, I felt a return to myself. Hidden within the rainforest, I found a way to sew regeneratively.

Between the mountains again, I helped my mum with a project, patchworking a huge quilt from fabrics she had collected over the course of her life. Watching her hands slowly join these old fabrics together with deep, colorful weaves, she taught me techniques that her mum had taught her. As the sun set, we went out to the garden, sowing seeds in the volcanic soil under the mountain. I dug my hands into the earth, planting a seed I had swapped with a neighbor. It grew, so slowly, spreading its leaves up to the sky. In my mum's sprawling garden, I saw that each bloom was filled with ancient knowledge and traditions passed down. Each seedling gave something back to the earth. Each seed held meaning.

The rainforest taught me to see fashion in everything around me. I saw my ancestor's knowledge in my dirty,

cracked hands. I saw the strong community of farmers in these hills. Mostly, I saw the symbiotic systems of the rainforest, working with harmonious reciprocity. I realized that fashion endlessly consumes resources while giving nothing in return, but I also understood it didn't have to be like this. Like gardening, fashion could be slow, considered, artful, and timeless. I could learn from ancient crafts, and each stitch could hold meaning, becoming a slow dance that moves to the rhythm of the seasons, myself, and the earth. Fashion could not just consume, it could regenerate.

In nature, I found the answers to everything. The rainforest's bowerbirds taught me color theory. The spiders' webs taught me to weave. The flowing waterfalls taught me to drape fabrics. And the fallen eucalypt's bark taught me to make intricate patterns to fit my body. Nature became my greatest teacher, and I was endlessly inspired by her creativity. My practice was shaped by these curling waters, rewoven by each graceful spider.

I started a big project that encompassed all I'd learned. Designing patterns for weeks, I perfected everything so that the dress I was constructing could fit flawlessly and be worn forever. I collected my

grandmother's old sheets, cutting around holes to make use of the beautiful cotton. On my studio floor, I worked for days, sleeping between sprawling pattern pieces and fabric scraps. My sewing machine broke as I sewed many delicate seams. To replace it, I bought a beautiful old machine that had been sewing magically for a hundred years. It solidified my belief that fashion hasn't always been like it is now. Once, machines were built to last and serve us for generations to come. Once, clothes told stories of self, culture, identity, and traditions.

I embroidered many flowers across the dress with my hundred-year-old embroidery machine. The artisanal technique seemed impossible at first since the old machine was awkward and jerky, but it guided me. Its handwheel was worn with generations of fingerprints, and mine fit into their aged hollows. Slowly, like a seedling in the garden, this dress grew. My creation didn't consume resources, but instead honored waste that already existed. I crafted with the knowledge of the rainforest, my ancestors, and the garden's soft blooms. My work wasn't confined by trends or consumerism, but was instead woven with timeless intention. Slowly, I created a dress that encompassed every part of my being.

HANDS, HEART, AND MIND

――――

Hands

Our hands have become wizened, lined with the stories of
our lives. Written into our skin are our work and
adventures, trials and joys. They hold wisdom and lessons
in each scar and crevice. In our daily life, we are always
using our hands as tools. We build, mend, dig, and chop.
But even in the most menial of jobs, we work with
diligence and a sense of grandeur. In each moment of our
daily life, we create artistic expressions depicted from our
innermost depths, and each task becomes a grand artwork.
We build the animals' night pens not just to safely house
them but to gracefully stand within the mountains. As we
shepherd and mend fences, we watch our work change the
landscape. We stitch, embroider, paint, harvest, prune, and
collect eggs. Our hands pull weeds and scatter seeds and
feel the land's gratitude for our care. As we work, we see
the convergence of each element of ourselves. Our hands
are busy, and we are immersed. Our minds are empty, and
we reflect inward. Our hearts are full, and we are whole.

Heart (Julia)

I walk along the rainforest path with a canvas tucked under my arm and an old wooden box of paints hanging heavily on my shoulder. The brilliance of unfurling ferns against the dark understory draws me in. Their spored hands reach for the touch of light. Further on, the ground becomes soft underfoot as I reach the water's edge. The sun sits low to the west. Dancing off the water, it bathes everything it touches in dripping orange light. This is the place my heart seeks, between the mango tree that reaches over the water and the age-old hoop pines that leave long shadows on the shifting grasses. I unfold my easel, propping its wooden legs in the mud and begin to paint. My hands work to my heart's guidance. Like an instrument to the land, I paint, conducted by my gratitude for its beauty. Strokes appear like the sun's last rays—anticipated and enchanting all at once. The water's reflections shift, but my strokes hold them encapsulated in time. Intuitively and like magic, the landscape flows onto the canvas.

Mind (Anastasia)

My mind is empty as I create; intention guides me. I move to its presence, and the world goes quiet. It is afternoon in the studio, and the sun shines on nothing but my workbench. As I work, the kookaburras' calls fade and the rumbling storm stands suspended in the sky. Every movement, motion, and being is still, and sewing becomes as ingrained as the bird's calls or the storm's falling rain. My scissors cut through fabric; their snips echo in the quiet of my mind. I patchwork pieces together, seams connecting through intuition. In mindless creativity, I sew each element of myself and see them connected in unison. My hands follow a silent rhythm, guided by my mind's intention and my heart's feeling. I find calm by externalizing my inner feelings and thoughts, spoken through the language of the hands.

ART PREACTICES

Earth as Art

See each sunrise as a grand painting and each sunset as an unseen expression from the earth. The empty sky is a blank canvas, and your empty mind is a vessel to be filled. Paint with the courage of the sky's bright pinks. Dance with the grace of the last light on the clouds. Learn from the earth's creative ways and fill each moment with art.

Step-by-Step

See your life like an artwork, your artwork like a life. Don't try to view it all at once; notice a convergence of many elements entwined. A portrait consists of a million tiny strokes. A life consists of a million tiny moments.

Tell Stories

See that stories are the simplest and strongest art— we are held by their verses. Weave stories throughout your life; share honest wisdoms, lessons, laughter, and hardships. Eternally pass knowledge through the great art of storytelling.

Perceive the World

See that in your perception lies your ability to create, to express, and to be. Inspect everything with creativity, and find meaning within the ordinary. Let your hands act as your eyes; they will guide you. See the world reflected in your making; your creations can write the truth of your visions.

Create Imperfectly

See perfection in the imperfect. Create for no reason but joy and perspective. Make messy paintings and sew faulty gowns, but feel the growth of each meaningless creation. Do not commodify craft, but instead enjoy the act of making.

Expression

See yourself expressed in everything you do; each action is signed by your name. Your life is a gallery of small interactions, so let your artistry be seen. Weave the ordinary with depth. Paint the darkness with beauty. Watch yourself reflected in everything you create.

The Art
of Learning

I climb the old mango tree for her wisdom,
my hands mirror her reaching branches.
There are infinite lessons held within these ancient arms:
her deep roots teach me that everything I need is already within me,
my ancestors' knowledge moves through me.
Her weathered bark teaches me that storms will come,
but they will move on, they smooth her.
Her curling flowers teach me to absorb all that I can,
there is knowledge and energy in each small moment.
Her bright fruit teaches me to give,
and feed the world with this simple wisdom.

NATURE'S EDUCATION

Fireflies are the first sign of summer. Down by the lake, where the tree ferns and palm fronds are a rich hue of shaded green, they emerge from the humus, cued by the lengthening days. They spend their short lives dancing and shedding light. These small insects weave meaning and connection, mate, then lay eggs—nestling in the earth the assurance of a future generation. There is an old cabin built down on the water's edge. We camp here all summer, and on moonless nights the fireflies blink around us, lighting the darkness with their intention.

This cabin was built by our dad. We watched him assemble it, working with such graceful ease. Its round beams still look like trees standing, held together with notches that were carved by his big hands or a swift, artful twist of the chainsaw. The tallowwood poles were felled from the edge of the orchard. Standing in place, we can still see their arms as part of the forest. A fork in the trunk is gracefully twisted so that it leans to support a rafter, and a branch is placed delicately to hold a lantern, as if it grew perfectly into place. Our summers were spent stripping bark from these trees, nailing floor boards, and sorting old iron. The roof is patched together from thousands of old pieces of tin that were once the roof of our hometown's movie theater, and then the leaky roof of our home. By the time the iron was repurposed for the cabin, it had more holes than tin. The constellations of old screw holes told us these stories as we slept under its shelter.

There is no place that feels more like home than this lake and the firefly-filled cabin on its edge. We have

been taught more by its waters than anything else: the days of swimming enfolded in its softness have shaped us. Here, where the water embraces you like silk, we would always swim out deep into the center of the lake, pausing in rapture at the beauty of the last golden light flickering to the west. Our childhood's most nurtured nights have been spent in the cabin's loft, with the ribcage of old beams holding us. Here we have been serenaded by frogs and owls and awoken with the morning sun dancing off the water. This place is the home of our hearts.

Time was endless in those long summers, and the crafting continued through months and years of learning. Together, our family built rafts and pontoons, flying foxes and rope swings that flung us higher and faster into the water than any kid could dream of. We built hot water systems heated by the fire and a little bathhouse perched over the stream, that was just strong enough to hold an old, clawfoot bathtub. Treehouses and platforms emerged in every treetop, carved by our dad's hands with the wood that grew on this spot. We would paddle across the lake; return with canoes filled with lychees, mangoes, and jackfruit; and

cook up a feast on the fire. With our grandparents and parents, aunties, uncles, cousins, and friends who became family, we'd play board games and tell stories around the fire—learning from the stillness of being as much as the endless creative energy of those summers. Working together, the skills of the generations grew within us. In this gift of sharing time, our elders showed us a way of being. It was a passing of knowledge of how to create and how to exist.

When our dad died, we camped down here once again. The roof was leakier than ever, and termites had found their way into the bathhouse. Without our dad's skills and stories, we didn't know where to begin. The immensity of all the knowledge we'd lost felt like a blow deeper than any other. We had not yet learned how to use the chainsaw or how to fell trees and craft beams into these grand and intricate structures. We'd only watched as our dad did this work. He was always so silent in his artistry. But, sitting with our mum—the structure above us like an arc of memories—she reminded us that he, too, learned the ways of a woodsman by himself. He knew what timber to use by watching the old banana farmers and how to craft it by looking up at the buildings around him. He learned how to use a chainsaw by trying, failing, and trying again. What he left to us wasn't necessarily skills, but rather the willingness to learn. Throughout his life, he showed us how to be a friend, how to love, how to create—but most of all, how to grow. Like a firefly on a moonless night, he shone his brightness where it was most needed.

THE WISDOM
OF NOT KNOWING
—by Anastasia

During the first few weeks after coming home from university in the city, I relished in the simplicity of the rainforest. I was tired from my routine of relentless study, and my body ached from long nights of pattern making and sewing to meet deadlines. For the past year in the city, I had been striving for success, and my creativity was guided by a distant goal of perfection. Returning home, I walked into the rainforest and sat under the pine trees, looking out to the lake below. A kingfisher swooped for fish and the forest's reflections shifted with symmetrical movement—a swirling mess of sky and trees and sunlight. The water's erratic fluidity taught me that nothing in nature is complete or perfect. The fluctuations, changes, and impermanence are what creates the beauty of the world.

All at once, my aspirations for perfection faded into those reflections, carried away by the ripples and motion of the water. I became empowered in the understanding that like nature, I, too, am perfectly incomplete and beautifully imperfect. This perspective taught me that aiming to understand everything is useless, that there is wisdom in not knowing. I wanted to experience the joy of trying something and knowing that I might fail, while also understanding that every step would teach me something new. Seeking knowledge and skills that once felt unachievable, I climbed up the hill and scavenged through my dad's old shed. It had been left untouched with the loss of his presence, each tool representing his wisdom and skills that we hadn't yet learned. With a few screws, a drill, and some hardwood, I went back to that spot above

the reflecting waters and started to build a wonky treehouse. My hands held the power to teach myself.

Every day, I walked to the water's edge and tried something new, challenging myself to learn a seemingly unachievable skill. My mum taught me how to use power tools, and a whole world opened up to me. I spent days trying to drill into hardwood, but the wood splintered and my screws broke. Understanding my ignorance, I asked my uncle for help, and he taught me that a simple pilot hole could let me drill with ease.

Every morning, before the sun rose, I would hike to a patch of invasive bamboo, cut it with a handsaw, and drag it down the steep hill. A flood came and it rained for days, but I kept hiking up that hill and carrying the long, heavy bamboo on my shoulders until I finally had enough to build the floor. Salvaging old ropes from around the farm, I tied all the bamboo together. My blistered hands instinctively wove a pattern that held everything in place. Each tiny step I'd taken led me to this moment, when my weeks of work became woven as one and a completed treehouse emerged.

I sat up on the platform with pride and watched over the same reflections, endlessly moving out across the water. My rough beams and broken screws reminded me again that nothing is perfect, but everything holds meaning. Humbled by the vastness of knowledge, I was curious of our endless ability to learn new things.

The wisdom of nature taught me to build and learn fearlessly, and I saw each day as a lesson. But soon, I was reminded of the earth's imperfect unpredictability when a storm came and knocked all my work down. The treehouse fell into the water and the reflections sat obscured by broken bamboo and mud. I stood amid the mess of my creation, overwhelmed by all that I did not know. I looked at this failure as something I knew I could grow from. The storm's wind had swayed the trees, and the pressure had broken the screws. Slowly, I planned out new systems so the treehouse could move with the trees. In this process of rebuilding and rethinking, I learned the most. I gained perspective in reconsideration, and soon I could see my failure as a tool for understanding more. By seeking knowledge, challenging myself, and moving with failure, I learned to learn again.

LISTENING
TO THE EARTH
—by Julia

The seasons spin around my slow life and teach me how to listen. I know every bird and the time of its song, movement, mating, migration, and return. The cusp of each season is coded in my memory. The way the sun slants through the trees reminds me that it is time to plant our winter garden, and the smell of the ripe lychees tells me that the rain will come soon. The kookaburras that sing at sunset every summer night are my calendar. These cues are a collection of diverse notes that form an atlas in my mind. They grow pathways of knowledge filled with planting calendars, harvest times, and seasonal guides.

I feed the sheep as the sun sets when the last light dusts the mountains. It is a time that is neither day nor night, when my instincts call me home. After the sheep are fed, I have a practice of sitting still for a moment, engulfed in the wideness of the sky with my bare feet touching the soft ground. It is my favorite time of day, and just as the sun slips under the tree line, my senses stir in the moment's stillness. I make a wish in the direction of Venus as she rises from where the sun has sunk beneath the horizon.

Here, where my mind floats with the endless sky above, I begin sketching. I watch the colors of the mountains and draw their shifting shapes. Each day, no matter what, I make a drawing. Sometimes they are small and free with tiny rough lines and feelings sketched expressively onto the page. On other days, they are more complex: like a fingerprint of my emotions and the day's shifting season. The freedom of this practice lets me see the world as enchanted. I draw like a child, boundless and

uninhibited—and in this, I learn to observe the undercurrent of life.

As I become consumed in my drawing, the last light quickly empties from the sky. No moon rises, and all at once, a blanket of velvety blackness covers both the rainforest and my senses. The calm of my mind is lost, too, as I imagine the walk home in darkness. Along the avenue of mango trees, through the gate, and down among the scrubby ferns into the deep rainforest gully, over the trickling creek, and up the hill—the journey with no torch and no moon to guide me seems unthinkable. Whether my eyes are open or closed, there is no difference in the darkness, so I begin stumbling down sheep tracks, thinking of snakes in the grass and spiders caught in my hair. But in the darkness, I let my mind become quiet once again, opening my senses to the world around me. I don't worry about the path ahead, but wander, guided by my imagination. I find the same strength I gain from the freedom of drawing: it is the ability to see like a child again, learning from the infinite wonder of the earth.

From the birth of my knowledge, my instincts awaken. Ferns brush against my legs as their touch directs me. The earth presses beneath my feet, communicating the way forward. Soft, spongy ground and wet stones tell me I've crossed the creek. Between the trees, a bright fungus glows; its bioluminescence lights the way. Like an ethereal marker, it guides me to turn right. I've reached the ferny bank, so I know it's time to begin the climb up the hill toward home. Crickets and frogs sing to the night's empty sky. I smell the cinnamon myrtles, and their sweet scent traces the hillside, leading me on. The stars become bright, shining between the fronds of a tree fern. Their infinite mystery hangs as a reminder in the sky—they let me understand all that I do not know. In darkness, I stop seeking to grasp each thing, but instead celebrate the beauty of the unknown. With a child's wisdom, I am open and curious, settled in the vastness of the universe. Tuned to the rhythm of the sun, moon, and stars, my heart opens to the innate knowledge of the earth. In joyous vulnerability, I feel my way home.

LEARNING TO OBSERVE

Banana plantations fill the top of the valley, nourished by the volcanic soils and hot sun. Under the cliff face we traverse the deep winding paths. Rough trails curve to the ancient crater's edge where a forest of bananas glisten in the golden light. We follow a farmer who we recently befriended as he proudly navigates his organic patch. His hands confidently machete the sappy stalks, and bunches fall into his arms with grace. He once knew our dad—who was a banana farmer too—and he learned from our dad's organic farming methods. They exchanged insights all those years ago, and now he teaches us all the lessons he has gathered. Knowledge that we thought was lost is now returned in bunches of the tastiest bananas. We learn about the life cycle of a banana plant which grows tall to produce fruit and then wilts and dies before being born again as small plants at its base. We see that knowledge is eternal too: it moves like energy, constantly passing, transforming, and rebirthing.

In modern farming, banana plants have been cultivated to be seedless, which means that each plant is propagated from cuttings that are almost genetically identical to one another. As they reproduce, they do not adapt, shift, or change. Because of this, they are under threat due to their lack of diversity. Disease threatens to wipe out whole varieties, and from this, we learn to never stay stagnant: to always learn and grow, shifting with ourselves and the earth.

Under the thick canopy of swaying banana leaves, we learn the art of observation. Our banana farmer friend teaches us how to adapt like the rainforest's deep roots,

and plant our gardens with the same intentional balance. He explains his carefully curated forest: sweet potatoes cover the bare ground and smother weeds while avocado trees reach deep into the soil's nutrients, holding and protecting the earth against landslides. In response to depleted soils and unpredictable rains, he has begun working with nature. The tall banana fronds dance joyfully above as he loads our arms with bunches of bananas, whose fruit is ripening fast with the coming full moon. He explains that banana plants move to the moon's cyclic rhythm. The fruit ripens quicker when it waxes, and banana corms transplant best when the moon is almost full. We all shift to the cycles of nature.

We wake to a new morning, inspired by the rising sun and the lessons of nature. In the north-facing slopes of our garden, we plant banana corms, carefully placing sweet potato cuttings at their bases. The ground cover will quickly spread, smothering weeds while keeping the soil wet and fertile. We plant the garden with intention founded in knowledge. This year's cabbages were eaten by moths, so we observe our mistakes and interplant dill and sage whose

fragrant scent will confuse pests. We watch worms and bugs and discover the soil's health from this delicate, balanced ecosystem. Energized by the warm sun on our faces, we work tirelessly to pull many weeds, and soon their piles tower over us. At this time of year the garden is magical. The last of winter's flowers stand firmly, but they will wilt and join the earth soon. In the forest's continuity, we observe that plants grow and die back, feeding the soil as they rot. From the banana plant's reproduction and the moon's eternal cycles, we learn that life rebirths and returns. The cycles of energy do not stop, they adapt and transform. So we haul the weeds to the compost, where they rot and quickly renew into healthy soil. Their energy feeds the earth and nourishes our seedlings' growth.

We learn from the garden's lessons and know that each seedling, worm, and tree can teach us something new. In the eternally shifting cycles of nature we understand that energy is constantly morphing. We see that knowledge also shifts with the earth's rhythm. Passed along, it sprouts, grows, wilts, and transforms.

GROWTH PRACTICES

Learn How to Learn

Know that everything you need is within you. Learning is ingrained within our minds, and growth is imminent. Like a heartbeat, our lives are conducted by our endless ability to learn. In the pulse of life's ongoing lessons, always shift, change, and grow.

Be Diligent

Know that you will find a path through practice. Below your feet are repetitive stones, but see that they lead onward to unimaginable places. Do not watch the faraway view, but tread carefully over the consecutive stones— move forward through each diligent step.

Return to Your Inner Child

Know that within you is the wisdom of a curious child: always creating, imagining, growing, and learning. Remember to view the world with a child's endless ability to learn as lessons hide within each moment. Open yourself to the knowledge of the universe.

All Growth is Growth

Know that in challenges there is growth. Even your mistakes are joined with knowledge, so let your stumbles lead you forward. A fruit tree blooms thousands of flowers; some blossoms become abundant fruit and some wilt in the sun. See the purpose in each of them.

Be Still

Know that a seed is silent below the earth. It can wait for years before its tiny sprout feels the sunlight on its leaves. Be still and know that growth awaits. Find perspective in the calm.

Observe

Know that knowledge is hidden everywhere. Observe the world around you, and uncover an invisible library. Read the pages of nature's lessons, analyzing the intricately woven systems. Study the books of connection, inspect each small thing, and find wisdom between the archives of life.

Creative Wisdom

*The shore's shifting waters
ebb before they flow.*

*Our constant breath in the wind
exhales before it inhales.*

*The instinctual dance of bees
pollinate before they feed.*

*Our gestures move to the rhythm of return:
to receive you must first give.*

SUSTAINABLE DESIGN

There was a half-finished farm shed on the hill above the lake. Its pine beams were exposed and skeletal—rotting in the sun, rain, and wind—still waiting to be protected by our dad's hands that would never come. We looked up to them: the soft grain of their wood fading like fingerprints against the blue sky. This place came to represent all that we had lost; the old tools around us were a painful reminder of the skills we had not learned. The rotting beams time-stamped this knowledge as it faded from the earth.

On this same ridge, our great-aunt Frieda once told us to look to the sky. She visited from the Netherlands almost once a year, timing her stays to the coming of fireflies, the red flush of flame trees, and the monsoonal rains. From her, we learned the joy and freedom of being, but on this night, she was somber. She called us little treasures in Dutch as she lay a blanket on the grass, pointing to the sky.

Smiling mystically, she told us that in the north sky there is a constellation in the shape of an axe. It lights the winter sky with the strength of its lines. Here in the southern hemisphere, she told us, it is different. The axe shines the most in the summer, in the time of fireflies and flame trees. She pointed to the brightest star. Our small hands followed the line of the axe's handle down to the blade. It hangs upside down here in the southern skies, she explained. With her arms extended, she showed us the spin of the earth around the sun: the way it tilts to make our seasons, why her wintertime is our summer, and why the axe twirls around us as the stars do, guiding our days.

Then, lying beside us, she told us the story of our family name. We were once people of the woods who saved a nobleman with the strength of our tools and were given a name to honor this—the name that means *of the axe*.

Thinking of this story years on, we looked up to the unfinished wooden frame. We imagined our dad up there—saddling a beam with a smile, carving wood, and letting a shower of sawdust fall meters below. He built in the way of the ancient woodsman. Felling trees to care for the forest, he used the materials available to him, crafting from wood and repurposed objects. He understood the spin of the world, and built to the sun's movement across the land. Our parents designed our family home to passively capture the warmth of the sun into its floor. Great windows face the north to allow the winter sun to enter and be absorbed into the building. More windows are placed to catch the wind, inviting its cool passage through the hallway and bedrooms. Verandas shade the western walls, and there are trees planted for shelter. There is no need for air conditioning among the cooled walls and no need for heating, except for a simple wood fire. We see now that this ancient knowledge of building with the environment is timelessly resourceful.

Under the shed's cathedral-like ceiling of rounded logs, we understood that the knowledge of the axe was in our father. He was never taught these ways, but must have learned from the guidance of our name. Knowing the axe constellation hangs above us in the sky, we realized that this wisdom must be within us too. And so, we decided to finish building the farm shed, renovating it to become an

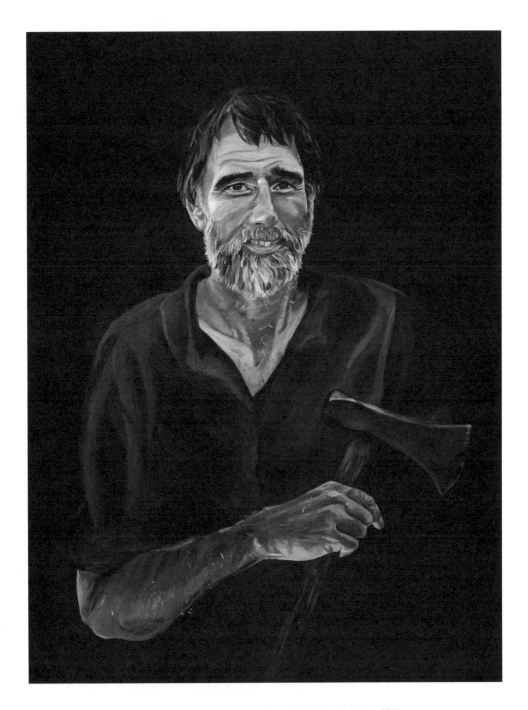

Portrait of our dad, John (Big Bird) Vanderbyl, *Man of the Axe*, 2016.

art studio, a place of creativity. Looking to the knowledge of the stars, sun, wind, and trees, we knew where to begin.

We found big, old windows that were being thrown away and placed them to the north so that the sweep of the low, winter sun would fill the room with its warmth. There were floorboards being sold as scrap from the mill. They were scarred with knots and holes and were difficult lengths, but we patched them together and sanded the timber over the course of days, laying out a sprawling floor mapped with character and meaning. We raised walls made from recycled hay and found more doors that had been destined for landfill. They opened to invite a cross breeze from the south. We roofed the weathered beams with old tin, collecting the rain that once rotted them. All the while, we felt an awakening of something within us. Our dad's old tools were being used once again, and the skills of the axe grew in our tired muscles. We found the ability to do anything.

HONORING THE ARTISAN

Within these mountains, threads of artisanal knowledge are laced through everything. An unspoken language of doing, creating, thinking, and making connects us all. There is a poetry of using our bodies directly with our thinking.

In university, we believed our education would teach us everything, but returning to the country, we looked to our neighbors' worn hands, and we realized that there was so much knowledge held in our community's palms. We understood the value of traditional skills, seeing the power of the knowledge passed down through farming, crafting, and this simple way of living.

We sat in our grandmother's garden as she picked her sprawling strawberries and fed us with their unimaginable sweetness. Once, we laughed at her scattered towers of pots and garden tools that held these strawberries up high above the wet ground and the passing grubs. Now, having returned home from the city, where the strawberries had tasted weak, we cherish them once more.

Our neighbor called to her cows, her voice echoing through the hills while the herd came running, catching the first light as they jumped over the creek. Her family members have been milkers for generations, and this role is instinctual to her being. In the shadows of the old bales, her arched body leaned against her favorite cow, their silhouettes curved to the shape of the mountains. Everything was still except for the movement of her hands and the abundant flowing milk. Afterward, she moved the cows to a new paddock, an ancient and almost forgotten practice that easily avoids worm burden and promotes more growth in the grasses.

Under the mountains again, our mum pointed out each tree and bird. We were once bored by this endless chatter, but now, our hearts were yearning to understand the differences between a tallowwood and yellow stringy eucalypt. We sought to know the reason why the spangled drongos sing in the spring and began to appreciate the wonder of a bowerbird's nest.

Looking at this community of makers and farmers, we learned the importance of generational wisdom, understanding that each person can teach us something. From them, we knew that there was more than one type of knowledge and more than one type of education. Like a handwoven blanket, the thread that connects these people is their fearless sharing—their proud, unwavering ability to teach us their skills.

They weaved a delicate lattice of lessons, stories, skills, and knowledge so strongly that the structure remains, even without their presence. One day, we found our oma's old hand tooled leather bag. She had carved it to be the shape of a rainforest leaf and engraved symbols of our family name onto it. She passed away when we were babies, but in the leather, we could still see the movement of her hands that carved the bag with stories of her life. Inside the bag were the tools of her trade: spools of thread, pattern-making equipment, and leather scissors. With these tools, we understood that we could still learn from her knowledge and teach ourselves these artful skills. The ability was within us all along, and we realized we could mend this connection once again. We learned to sew, mend, and pattern make, feeling her knowledge pass through us.

ANASTASIA: *I found a worn square tablecloth embroidered with delicate flowers. It was made in another era, so intricate and detailed—but over time it had filled with stains and holes. I decided to challenge myself and find a way to utilize each inch of this beautiful creation, designing a blouse that honored its broken wholeness. I cut tessellating triangles from this stubborn square, careful not to waste a single warp or weft. But in my contrived cuts, I had to make sure to avoid stains and holes. I snipped its threads carefully, aware of the meaning each fiber carried. The negative space became as crucial as the rest. I used pin tucks to shrink a pattern piece and calculated flare to extend another. I utilized the*

entirety of the tablecloth, meticulously mosaicking these precious scraps together, creating a blouse that held every story.

It was only when I focused inward to design this impossible top that I noticed the layers of hand stitching. The tablecloth had been mended several times. Embroidered petals had unraveled but had been replaced in an almost identical thread. Some holes had been carefully darned and covered. In these layers of woven histories, I felt the force of the women before me. Their power and knowledge were like hands guiding my own. Threads of meaning were stitched between those seams. The thread seemed to sign their names, and with my new stitching, I signed mine too.

THE BEAUTY OF IMPERFECTION

In the orchard across the lake and over the hill, the mango trees are full. It is autumn: the time of abundance when the blue shadows begin to stretch and the trees are dripping with bright fruit. We walk to the mango trees planted by our parents with a fruit picker in our hand and goats by our side. Valencia pride, nam dok mai, and golden, these varieties' names are as beautiful as their soft curves. With the help of the picker to reach the highest fruit, they fall gently into our hands. The sap drips, and we distract the goats by offering them a nearby Malay apple. We can all smell the succulence of the mangoes' golden flesh.

Next, we twist under the persimmon tree and the lychee's drooping branches. They are heavy with fruit that showers into our basket as we pull at their stiff stems. Past the jaboticaba for a juicy snack, we reach our favorite jambu tree. Its fruit is the brightest of all the jambu on the farm and spreads a blanket of pink beneath the tree. Juicy like a watermelon, crunchy like an apple, and rich like a berry, a jambu picked straight from the tree tastes like nothing else. In the paddock, with the sun setting over the hill, it feels as if we can taste the last of summer in its waxy flesh. When this tree gifts us with her abundance, there is more fruit than leaves, and we race to catch their delicate ripeness before they fall to the ground. The second that jambu are harvested, their fragile nourishment begins to rot. We rush home with full baskets, and across the kitchen table, we spread a tapestry of green mangoes, jambu, and Malay apples. With the temporality of their beauty urging us on, we begin chopping and salting. Little

bruises are flecked through their flesh, and we cut around them, knowing that each fruit covered with imperfections is equally filled with nutrients.

We step out the screen door into the garden where papayas hang heavy above us and star fruit cluster on branches that hang over the asparagus ferns. Climbing the tall, straight trunk of the papaya tree is always a struggle, but with a twist and a click, the bulging fruit drops into our hands. We see that the papaya's skin is speckled with tiny black dots, and mold is starting to grow in her pores. The fruit won't ripen before the mold makes it to their insides, so we innovate and pick baskets of green papayas, peeling and finely chopping their chalky green flesh to turn into the most-delicious ferments. We dig turmeric and ginger from the garden, pluck chilies from their bushes, and back in the kitchen, we mix them all in with the jambu. Weaving layers of salt, our hands massage this wondrous mix of bright fruit. Our mum joins in with big, old pottery bowls. This is when the three of us crush and knead the salted fruit into shining jars, laughing as their juice splatters up our arms. Mum pulls out an old recipe

book. On the faded page, framed by similar splatters, is a handwritten recipe. It is as poetic in its practicality as the three of us are, laughing while we work around the kitchen table. It is our neighbor, the cow farmer's recipe; she is like a grandmother to us and was taught this recipe by her grandmother. Passed through the hands of the women of these hills, the recipe teaches us how to preserve chokos and green fruit into sweet mustard pickles. We cut into the mangoes' green cheeks and follow the instructions like a song. A little sugar, a little vinegar, and some golden turmeric, rich and sweet.

The tall jars of fermented produce fill us with pride. They sit, pink, orange, and shining on our pantry shelf, capturing the colors and tastes of autumn for future meals. A bucket of scraps is left for the animals or the compost, as every part of each fruit has a place in the art of preserving. We see it as wholeness, a bottling of nature's effortless circularity. With our hands, we can honor this endlessly shifting imperfection and acknowledge that together, all broken things can make a whole. Every bruised fruit has something to give.

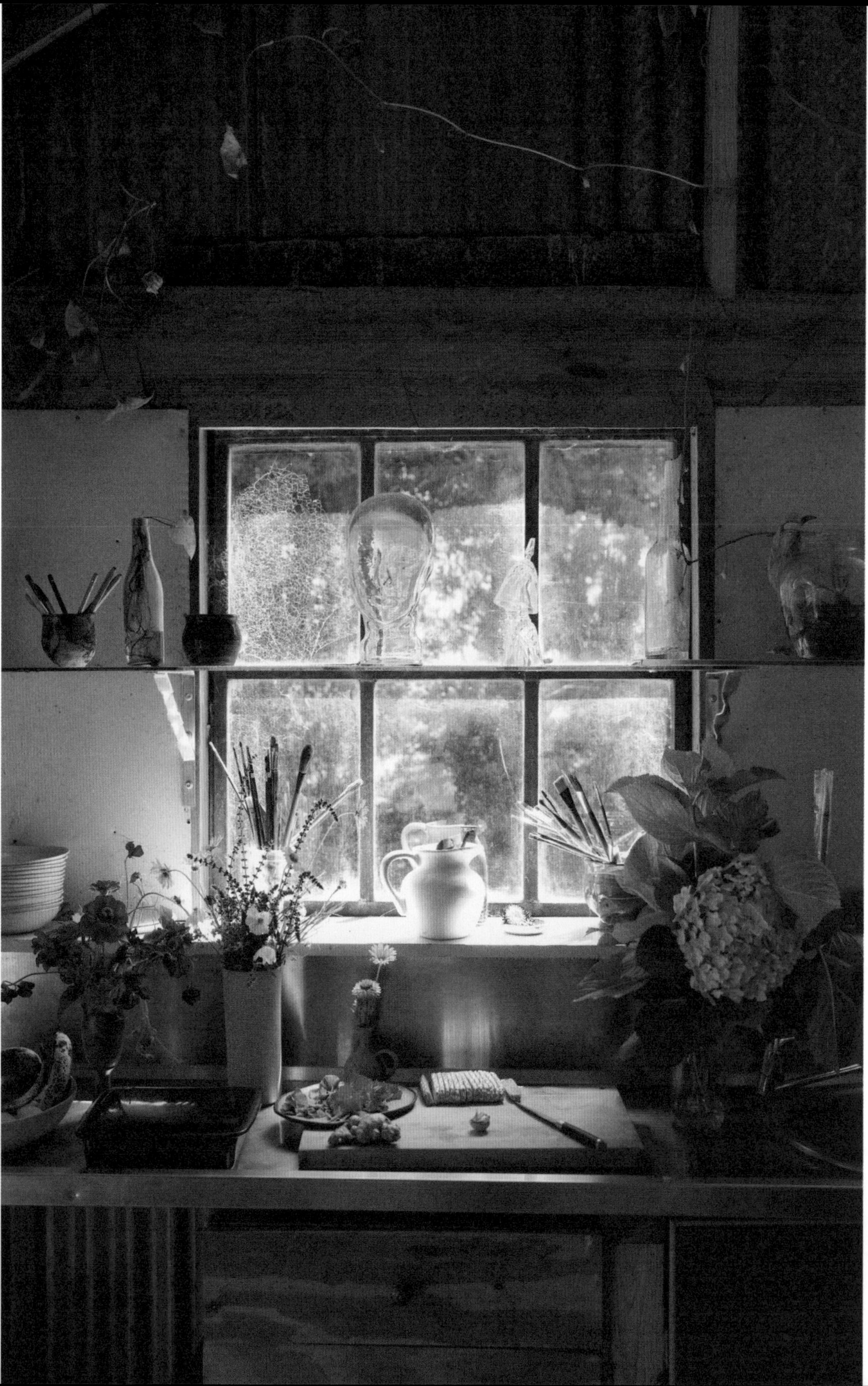

We think of the previous generations' innovations—freezers filled with browning bananas, baskets of collected fabric scraps, and delicately mended crochet blankets—and see it's only recently that humans hold the belief we can endlessly consume. In that old frugality, there was a determination of seeing potential in everything. We must learn to respect finite resources as sacred gifts from the earth and see the capacity to reuse and mend in each small thing. As our world shifts under the threat of the changing climate, this mindset becomes even more necessary.

There is joy in a zero-waste perspective. It is the understanding that imperfection, mended cracks, and rotting fruit fill our lives with meaning. The flawed and incomplete make the beauty of the world. We look around our childhood home at the foot of the mountains and see this way of living everywhere. Our fireplace is built from faulty bricks: a possum crawled over them as they dried, and their tiny paws are forever etched in the clay. Our mum lead-lighted the windows from scraps of glass collected from everywhere. The floor is a mosaic of old floorboards gathered from local demolished pubs, the post office by the sea, and the old cinema.

By celebrating the complexity of each object, we accept the natural cycle of things. Fruit rots, wood ages, and pottery breaks, but all flaws have meaning. We weave this knowledge into everything we create—art, food, homes, and clothing—understanding our lives as the sum of what we create and what we consume. We are what we leave behind; let it not be waste, but knowledge. Let our impact be stories and recipes, skills and beauty.

CREATING MORE
THAN WE CONSUME

Like magic, nature is in a constant rhythm of creation. The rainforest's systems work in perfect symbiosis: each element gives and receives, creates and consumes. The quandong tree absorbs nutrients and water and then drops thousands of tiny seeds. Some feed the soil, and some feed the birds, but the forest hopes that just one will grow into a tall, strong tree. We learn from nature's cycles of creation that we must return all that we receive from the earth through the gifts of our actions and art.

The quandong's blue seeds spread hope beneath the canopy, although there are other seeds within the forest who hold destruction in their growth. The camphor laurel is an introduced species that grows deep in the rainforest. Behind the enchantment of its huge trunk and glistening leaves, there lies a threat. Their invasive growth smothers native plants, and they consume the forest with no gratitude for the soil that feeds them. There are toxins within their leaves that seek to restrict the growth of native bush, taking koala habitats and biodiversity with them. Before the camphor laurels were introduced, native coolamon trees lined the waterways. The coolamons' deep roots held creek beds in place, and they grew with reciprocity for the rainforest that held them. But, choked by the incessant growth of camphor laurel trees, the coolamons' strength has been replaced with the camphors' shallow roots which lead to erosion. Lessons are written within their invasive leaves and poisonous seeds. These trees take endlessly from the ecosystems while giving nothing in return.

Our lives on this earth are etched with the fact that we all leave something behind, our impact spreading like seeds. With each action, we decide whether we are growing seeds of hope or seeds of destruction, giving or taking, creating or consuming.

ANASTASIA: *When I sew, I see each fabric, button, and thread as potential beauty for the future. Through a regenerative mindset, I work with material in the same way that we work with the land: by considering its previous histories while shaping its future. Even the smallest scraps or most-broken dresses are woven with hidden potential. To see the path forward, I always look back first; I imagine the stories held in each simple thing. It is here that I find the answers of how I can create beauty from waste and how my designs can transcend time.*

Regenerative agriculture works to this simple way of thinking by creating soils and nutrient-dense food without consuming endless resources. Cover crops and interspersed plantings are fed by the land while they return nutrients to the soil. The way animals interact with the earth is the key to this system. They give endless love to us and the land. As they eat weeds, eliminate invasive species, and repair soil health, they are nourished in return. The hope they instill in their intuitive care spreads, and we learn to follow the guidance of their generosity. Regenerative living repairs

The making of *The Dragonfly Dress*; days of pattern making, draping, cutting and sewing in the studio.

the mistakes of the past by always abiding to the simple philosophy of creating more than we consume.

Like the quandong tree, the crops, or the animals, we, too, have something to offer the world. We can make change with our art or knowledge, planting seeds and watching this meaning sprout in others. Living a life in tune with nature, creativity becomes the vessel through which we give to the world.

We let this way of thinking guide us, and slowly, we collect skills. Gathering lessons from nature, our elders, our diligence, and our failures, we find that we can learn anything. Our creativity becomes a natural dance. Every small action builds to create an organic flow. In the meditative process of creating, we feel a tide move through us. We understand the satisfaction of making change with our hands, and we feed on the return of accomplishment, perspective, and meaning. From this, we know that we must continue the ebb to this flow and give this back to the world.

It is our duty to become the teachers of our crafts, to share our knowledge fearlessly, and to pass on all the lessons we gather. Like the quandong tree, we receive sun, air, and water, and we give our seeds back to the world. We let them scatter and sprout, grow, and then make seeds of their own. Slowly, we grow a forest.

INTUITIVE PRACTICES

Flow

Feel the water. It rushes and cascades, but it also trickles and wavers. It moves through the land knowing it can take many paths. The water understands that whether it flows over the falls or seeps under the rocks, it will soon evaporate, becoming the clouds and the rain. Like water, flow with aimless intention and purposeful drift.

Seek Knowledge

Feel deeply and know that you do not know everything. The pursuit of every answer is insatiable, but each question asked brings new knowledge. Listen gently and find that you can learn something from anyone. Look softly and see the wisdom woven through each simple thing. Feel deeply and find hidden knowledge within yourself.

To Learn and to Teach

Feel your knowledge weighed with your duty to teach. The coolamon tree drops many seeds, and slowly, with nourishment from the summer rains and winter sun, a seedling emerges. A tree grows, a flower blossoms, and a fruit falls. Slowly, it all happens again. See knowledge as your seed; your growth is fed by lessons. Let yourself slowly transform from a small sprout to a grand tree, and know when it is time to drop your own seeds, becoming the passer of knowledge.

Find Strength

Feel the undercurrent of knowledge beneath your skin. Know the strength to achieve anything is within you. All of nature's elements grow with the collective understanding that small steps move toward great change. Follow your intuition.

Perspective

Feel perspective return. Release your whole self to your art; empty your mind, and find that it can be filled with the depth of the universe. Feel the power of your hands creating and the sensitivity of your heart's visions arising. In the convergence, see creativity shine like the first sun illuminating the land, and let it guide you.

Beauty in the Broken

Feel the layers of knowledge within each simple thing, understanding the beauty and potential of the broken. A torn dress sewn together again creates an intricate work of art, detailing stories within its repaired seams. See yourself not as broken, but with the potential for new stories to be threaded through your scars. See the earth not as fractured, but as the canvas for a better future. With hope, we can create changes that move beyond mending the climate's wounds. We can use our actions to create a world better than before.

PART III

CARE

*"We feel what it means to care for the
forest of an unknown future, and we walk
through the landscape with pride."*

Self and
Earth as One

See the mountains as our own flesh,
the rivers as our own tears.
Their peaks are burnt with fire,
their valleys are broken by flood.

But the sun still rises over their skin,
its familiar embrace holds us.
The moon still sets between their eyes,
its whispers reveal hidden ways.

On the edge of broken soil,
vines stretch like thread connecting seams.
On the scars of ashen ridges,
seeds burst like hopeful drops of ink.

See yourself as the earth,
and the earth as yourself.
See the vines as our own hands,
and the seeds as our own hope.

SEASONS OF THE SELF

———

Our lives are conducted to the tune of nature. Each moment is etched within cycles: joy and sorrow, death and rebirth, calm and turbulence. We look to nature and see ourselves mirrored back; the seasons of our life are as transient as the summer mist or winter shadows. Devastating storms will pass. Warm sun on our face will fade. The earth's wonder is woven between fleeting scenes so we learn to see beauty in each moment. Through nature's eyes we see the seasons of the self; our ever-changing lives dictated by fluidity and change.

Spring

The earth is dry; it is waiting. When the first storms come, everything resets in a magnificent rebirth of the land. Hidden seeds show themselves, awakening with the rain. Our minds are a spring landscape too—with water and sun, gratitude and understanding, we feel a colorful garden blossom into life. Everything starts from a small seed, even the largest trees and the most-beautiful flowers—it all begins below the soil, waiting for the perfect time to sprout. Our own hopeful seeds of knowledge and intuition rest just below the surface, hungry for growth, but calm in the stillness.

Summer

Deep growth echoes across the rainforest. The garden is an organized scramble of plants interlaced in movement: weeds woven through flowers, hot sun washed away by heavy rains. We learn from the energetic growth, but from the fierce weeds too. We clear the garden of our minds by tending the flowers and weeding everything else. Our care is embodied in our hands' considered movements. We embrace growth and our seedlings stretch toward the sun.

Autumn

The trees are heavy with bright fruit. Ideas to fruition, we harvest. We savor the tastes of accomplishment, nourished by the deep flavors of satisfaction. We share the fruits with neighbors, spreading recipes, preserves, and stories of our harvests. In connection, our understanding grows. Held in the support of community, we learn compassion; that everything is best when experienced together. So we share abundant kiwis as well as our ideas, hardships, joys, or burdens.

Winter

The days are shorter, and slow sunsets sweep through the mountains. The garden goes to seed in a glorious display of rotting vegetation. The fruit trees sit still in silence. We know that their roots extend under the earth as far as the canopy. Hidden in darkness, they are outstretched, collecting nutrients. If we nurture the soil of ourselves, we feel growth in the furthest branches. Compost created from waste, we see that everything has a purpose. Each stage of growth is beautiful; nature's decay creates fertile soils. In the stillness of hidden roots, the night sky, or fallen seeds, we know that we, too, must rest. The creek eases on these short, dry days. We must stand still to see our reflection in its waters. In rest, we see everything mirrored back to us.

GRATITUDE

Most summers bring energetic cyclones. They build out at sea and linger above the mountains as they move inland. In the intensity of these storms, we see the beauty of nature in all her forms. Thick clouds sit suspended over the caldera with endless rains falling from their depths. But in the eye of the cyclone, there is calm. Between the ferocity, the sun shines and an incomprehensible brightness grows. Pearly mist spreads through the valley, pink sunsets glow, and violet-tinged lightning streaks the sky. Intermittent sunlight creates rainbows in the mist, circling like a halo above the mountain. A cyclone's destructive beauty reminds us of the incredible gift it is to perceive: to see the dancing mist, smell the petrichor, feel the mud-covered earth, hear the ducks' joyful quacks, or taste the depth of the garden's harvest.

During a break between the heavy showers, we go to the garden and admire the grand beauty of every fleeting moment. In the stillness, we become entranced by each new stalk and petal. We are grateful for the sun who nurtures the plants and for the rain who feeds the soil. Our hands weave seeds through the ground to repay the earth with meaning. The seeds grow and feed us with their nourishment. Gardening is an endless cycle of appreciation, reciprocity, and regrowth.

In these brief moments between storms, we garden, as ducks play at our muddy feet. They waddle between the snapdragons and catch grasshoppers in their beaks, proudly quacking with joy. When they get tired, they nap in a sunflower's shadow and then shuffle off to their pond for a swim. For them, each moment is filled with joy.

We've learned to garden with a duck's awe: to rejoice in the beauty of a new bloom, to giggle at the feeling of mud between our fingers, and to plant cosmos just for fun.

The ducks splash in the muddy pond with water beading off their feathers. But Bee, the smallest duck, watches from the bank. Her oil gland never developed, so she isn't able to waterproof her feathers. We have tried everything from bubble baths to making her a custom raincoat, but her feathers are still heavy with dirt. When she was a duckling, we were told that without her natural insulation, she wouldn't survive, but three wet summers later, she still sits on her favorite warm rock and watches her friends play.

These days of intense rain and fleeting sun are difficult for Bee, so we care for her closely. The cyclone hovers between the mountains, and we see a shower approaching from the north with a heavy blanket of rain curtaining the view. It comes closer, and each familiar hill is cloaked from sight. The first heavy drops fall into the flowers, and we begin to run inside, leaping over bushes and between hedges. At our feet is Bee, who knows this routine well. She weaves through our steps and quacks at the sound of our laughter. We carry her inside and place her in a cardboard box by the window. She sits quietly and warms herself for hours.

We look at this duck and understand that she is thankful for each day, for the cyclones and the warm sun. Through her eyes we have learned to be unconditionally grateful. In the beauty of a destructive storm or the resilience of a tiny duck, we understand this life is a gift. This is where healing begins. In our appreciation, we begin to tend the soft seeds of a better world. Our care grows from them, and soon a deep bond sprouts, grounded in gratitude. We nourish the soils that feed us and protect the trees that give us their fruit. This way of being shows us how to nurture the earth that nurtures us.

ENVIRONMENTAL WELLNESS
—by Julia

After a storm, we see the echoes of its touch in the landscape. Sometimes, the creeks wash away their banks, palms are uprooted, and trees fall on fences. We spend months repairing, rebuilding, and replanting. In the worst storms, the land cracks, revealing slips of broken earth. It happens on ridges where the fires have burned and there are no root systems left to hold these dangerous rains. When I first became sick, I viewed my body like this: a torn battleground. My health was imbalanced and broken; there were no root systems to anchor it in place. But, just as I have come to love this wounded earth, that still holds us, I've learned to love my body as if it were a rainforest. Both strong and delicate, they are eternally imperfect. I watch vines and groundcover blanket exposed earth and I see myself as an extension of this—holding my flaws and wounds with the gentle compassion in which nature holds hers. I see the way she still thrives despite the turmoil of disaster, and I carry this hope within my body too. My health is like a delicate ecosystem, soft and powerful. Like the earth, it can find its way back to balance.

When I became chronically ill, I was forced to come to terms with the limits of myself far too young. I was only twelve years old when I was diagnosed with ME/CFS. Each day, I survived with a fraction of the energy of those around me. But I saw that nature has her limits too. We push at her boundaries every day, endlessly extracting from her resources. The effect of this is clear in biodiversity loss and degenerated ecosystems. Winters are hotter, and summers are drier. Nature's need to rest is illustrated in these escalating extremities. In our journey of

regenerative living, I've learned to give back against this tide of taking. I nourish the rainforest in small acts of compassion: sowing seeds, planting trees, and caring for animals. But I have also learned to give back to myself, to rest and never expect that I can extract from myself in the same way that we endlessly take from nature. Her imbalance is our own dysbiosis. Our health is tied to the earth's health in more ways than we can fathom.

Magnolia the goat was just a tiny baby when she came to the farm. It was early in our journey, when we were just beginning to see the patterns of nature's recovery across the land. Ecosystems were quietly being restored, and we realized that this healing was linked to the animal's care. So, we adopted Magnolia and her sister Moth from a farm over the mountain range. Magnolia's mother didn't have enough milk to feed her—weak and frail, she was barely surviving. Moth was older and fiercely protective of her younger sister. But one day, Magnolia sat her tiny body on my lap, and in this moment, an everlasting bond formed between us. She was fragile, but we cared for her, and day by day, she grew stronger. She became a big, gentle goat who follows me everywhere I go and sings back to me when I call her name.

Each day, Magnolia reminds us of the miracles of reciprocity, and we watch her thrive with such pride. She forages the hills for nutrient-dense fodder, nibbling on weeds and deep-rooted scrub that draws minerals from the soil below. Each diverse plant offers different nutrients, and Magnolia instinctively knows which will nourish her. Through her, we see nature's systems

interacting as a whole. As she grazes, her paddocks of regenerating grasses, forests, and bush are finding balance in wild biodiversity. We continue shepherding the goats through the hills, watching in awe as they heal the soils and delicate systems of life. From these healthy soils grow nutrient-dense vegetables, grasses, and fruit for both us and Magnolia. We are all fed by this bounty grown of rich earth.

Magnolia has now become a mother, passing the chain of care onward. Initially, her baby would only drink from one teat and her udder became swollen and full. I milked the other side, and now, every morning, Magnolia comes running through the gate toward me, eager to share the abundance of her milk. She jumps on her milking stand, and I nestle into her side. With my ear so close to

her fur, I can hear the turn of her stomach and the soft sounds she makes as she eats from a bucket of feed. The magic of her milk is suddenly so clear to me—just the day before it was the grasses and shrubs, and before this it was the sun and soil. Now, it is warm milk in a jar in my hands, and as I drink it, I feel the wholeness of nature's systems. I see the path toward balance. My actions of care for Magnolia extend to the land. Her grazing helped the rainforest return to health, and in its wholeness, it gave her what she needed to survive. Now, fed by rich, biodiverse shrubs, Magnolia passes this health back to me with her nourishing milk. We are all connected: from soils to human health and food systems to the environment's balance. My wellness is tied to the health of the earth and the animals. As they heal, I heal too.

CO-EXISTENCE

In early spring, all creatures awaken. The landscape is alive, and it shifts with change in each moment. The days are dry, but by the water, everything breathes with life. The frogs' chorus fills the warming air, and the dragonflies dip in the golden stream. There is a huge goanna, a lizard as big as a tree trunk—his claws hungrily shake bark to the ground as he climbs in search of a bird's nest. The currawong swoops to protect her eggs, tiny against his Cretaceous arms.

We walk carefully around the goanna and past the lake's edge to the orchard paddock where the goats are waiting for us, ready to come home in the fading sun of spring. At this time of year, the snakes are sleepy and slowly waking. This is when they are most dangerous, half-awake and lying in the sun's warmth. They are surprised easily and could bite anyone who accidentally steps on their still bodies. Early spring is no time to walk barefoot, but we have learned to live with them—stomping through the long grass and yelling *hello, snakes*—the vibrations warning them of our presence.

We find the goats waiting in the avenue of mango trees. As we join them, each goat looks up and greets us in their own distinct way. The flock are our kin. We move with them through the seasons: herding, resting, milking, and nurturing, deeply attuned to their movements and needs. All day, we have listened to the sound of their calls across the farm: Magnolia's call to her baby or Moth's soft disgruntled cry as she is distracted by a guava tree and left behind by the flock. Constantly alert, we tune our ears to hear if any of them are in trouble. The rainforest is a difficult place to survive; it is filled with hungry predators and hidden threats. Here, there lives the world's most venomous snakes, goannas, hawks, and eagles with a huge nine-foot wingspan who are strong enough to carry off a little goat, duck, or chicken in their taloned grip. But these ferocious predators are beautiful too, and their presence is so strongly linked to the health of these forests. Their roles are just as important as ours are, and we try to always remember this as we graciously live alongside these creatures.

We walk home with the goats to what was once called Death Adder Ridge. It was named for one of the most venomous snakes in the world: the death adder, whose short, scaly bodies were once found everywhere through the mulch of this forest. When he was a kid, our dad would dodge them with his bare feet, but in our lifetimes, we have never seen one. A death adder bite will leave you paralyzed. Despite their danger, we still mourn the loss of their presence. Without them, the ecosystem is imbalanced. The fragile threads of its weave snap as each delicate but integral species disappears from this earth. In our dad's youth, an introduced species of poisonous toads came to the rainforest, and within years, almost every death adder died from their poison. In the death adder's absence, there is a potent lesson: a reminder to protect all creatures, honoring biodiversity above all else.

ANASTASIA: *While the death adder is gone, there is a whole family of incredible snakes that exist alongside us. When I walk through the garden, I am always aware that it is the brown snake's home. Her bite would kill us in minutes, but we live in companionship, peaceful beside her power. There is the drainpipe where the big carpet python sleeps and the grapevine where the night tiger snake lives. I walk over the step where the little whip snake is curled and drink my morning coffee in the shade of the night tiger's grape vine. The snakes respect us, and we respect them. It is their home as much as ours.*

The springtime is full of new life, but it is also when these predators are hungry and waiting for their next meal, so we care for the goats closely during this time. One spring, Moth the goat gave birth to twin kids. Fragile and innocent, they were small enough to be held in an outstretched palm. Moth is the fiercest mother goat, and raising these tiny babies in the rainforest is a formidable feat. With so many watching predators, it was hard for her to care for herself while also making sure her babies were safe.

JULIA: *On a spring morning, I sat with Moth and her newborn babies. The kids jumped on my lap, bouncing and playing, falling asleep in the folds of my skirt. As they slept, cradled by my arms and the soft sun, Moth began to walk away. She got to the forest's edge and looked back at me, emotionally communicating in her gentle baa. With her innocent babies in my lap, I replied to her, softly explaining that I could look after them while she left to eat. She let out one final call and then walked off into the bush, slowly disappearing into the rainforest. Hours later, she returned with her belly full. Her babies bounced joyfully back to her, and this soon became a daily routine. Moth was hungry and tired, so she asked me to babysit every chance she got. Sometimes she came to our front door, kissing each tiny kid's head and then my knee or shoulder before trotting off to forage in the bush. In our care, Moth's babies grew alongside the snakes and hawks to become strong goats that now navigate the forest with such certainty.*

In Moth's trust, we see the strength of this soft life lived harmoniously alongside all creatures, as one with the snakes and goannas, the grasses and trees. Our relationship extends much deeper than shepherd and goat, or human and animal. In the years that we have spent keeping her safe, she has come to trust us in an unspoken bond. Our care has developed into a sacred friendship.

Animals have a way of speaking, a deep source of wisdom that reminds us that we are their kin. Nature is a web of interconnected beings, and in our responsibility to each of them, a rich relationship of reciprocity forms. Every animal's role is a strand in this web, singular but integral to the structure of life. We exist within these systems, intangibly connected to the weave of the world.

NURTURE PRACTICES

Be Nature

Listen to the birds sing, the frogs call, the wind's voice, and the stream's rhythm. Know that you are not separate from nature. We are all guided by the same water, orchestrated by the same moon. The sun's same beams fall onto our skin and the air's same breath feeds us. Walk with the earth, and feel the interconnections beneath your feet.

Rest

Listen to the earth's intangible patterns, and learn to recognize the seasons of yourself. Like a seedling, grow at your own pace. Move to the seasons of rest and the seasons of creation. Shift with shadows and brightness as the moon does: sometimes its face sits engulfed in darkness; sometimes it reflects bright light. Watch the cycles move on and find comfort in their rhythm.

Quieten

Listen to the slow rhythm of the earth. In silence, we hear our own thoughts meander like the stream. In stillness, we see the movement of our own reflection. In the smallness of being, we feel the vastness of the world.

Become Enchanted

Listen to your heart's whispers; it knows that to exist is a wonderful thing. Understand that your senses are a gift, and use them to see each ordinary moment as magic. See the beauty of nature, and sing songs back to the earth through the practice of gratitude.

Sit Still in Change

Listen to nature's teachings, and understand that nothing is constant. Each fragment is forever moving in light, shifting in the seasons, growing and wilting with time. The only constant is inevitable change. In stillness, see the beauty of this.

Co-exist

Listen to nature's cry. See her rainforests as skin, her mountains as flesh. Witness as our destruction leaves unimaginable scars, understanding that as nature crumbles we do too. Feel the earth's wounds, and in the depth, see that your ability to comprehend such sorrow shapes your ability to hope. See that if nature thrives, we do too.

The Weave
of the World

Time is a river, it flows when no one is watching.
My body is carved to the shape of its stones,
my mind mirrored in its shining waters.
But two rivers converge,
one holds all that has been,
and one holds all that will come.
Their confluence creates a pool of shifting reflections,
I bathe in the truth of its movement.

THE PRESENT MOMENT

A constant growth stretches from the rainforest's depths. Entangled are massive trees, insects, vines, snakes, marsupials, and bush. But between the deep, blue shadows that reach across these valleys, the pace slows. Far below the towering canopy, shifting sunlight passes gently. It falls from high above and impossibly moves through leaves, palms, and ferns, landing on the forest floor.

After the flood, the forest's turmoiled soils were rifted open. Trees fell and stories from beneath the earth seeped through cracked crevasses. Under the stretching canopy, an old rubbish tip was revealed, spilling out across the ground. There were old yogurt containers, engraved with dates and logos, from our dad's childhood, buried and unchanged for the last 50 years. Surrounded by the perpetual plastics of the past, we were shown that we are responsible for every small thing that we bring into the world—our impact is forever stitched into the earth. Our lives are fleeting, but our waste is permanent.

The plastic littered the ground, and the rain began carrying it down toward the creek. From here, it would make its way to the ocean. The birds began collecting it, and the rubbish continued degrading and leaching into the soils. So we spent weeks in the forest, collecting the scattered waste, sorting mud from plastic bottles, and untwirling bread wrappers from tree roots.

With our hands in the soil, we looked up to the gap in the forest's canopy. At our feet the bare earth was free. To heal the ground, we decided to plant a bunya pine sapling, imagining a grand tree that would one day reach across the sky. Its branches would fill the canopy and its

roots would spread through the soil, stitching the broken earth together. Bunya pines are ancient trees that can live for a thousand years. Their wizened bark curls between nodules, shaping eyes that watch over the forest.

In the potential of this bunya pine's immense life, we saw a glimpse of the future while the bags of old plastics at our side revealed the weight of the past. Between them, we understood the insignificance of our lives in the vastness of time. Our lives are small, but our impact spreads beyond our short existence.

We placed the small bunya pine sapling in the soil, wondering what it would see in its lifetime. In a thousand years, what elements of ourselves will still be woven into the land? Will it be the trees we plant or the waste we create, the knowledge we spread, or the wounds we pass? What we give and what we take will be inscribed in the earth.

As we watered the tree, massaging its roots with our fingers, we weaved our intention into the forest. We sat and breathed; the future landscape was already taking form in our hands. Nature shifted before us, and we watched with pride as a butterfly passed; its wings caught in a shaft of light, refracting unimaginable shades of deep blue. In its short lifetime, it pollinates flowers and creates beauty. We saw the importance of its insignificance and the change it creates during its fleeting life. Inspired by the power of the present moment, we understood that like the butterfly—our short lives can be spent making significant change in small actions of care.

As slow as a rainforest shadow, as still as a bunya pine, or as intentional as a swallowtail butterfly, time ceases to exist. The past becomes a lesson. The future is just a vision. The present is a needle, a tool to connect to the earth and thread meaning through our lives.

CHILDLIKE WONDER

After a thousand slow mornings under the mountain, the present moment stretches like a shadow from its peak. It spills over our lives, filling every moment with promise. The rhythmic tedium of each day is the same: we work and shepherd and create and grow. In this slowness, our minds carve space to reflect. We notice the smallest shifts and subtle seasonal changes, the way a fern catches the light or the first of autumn's fruit. In boredom, our minds meander like a stream and uncover glistening understanding. Connections unfurl before us. We see the secret of slowness—a way of living that extends time— and discover that the key to this timeless life is simple: it is to live like a child.

Our great aunt Frieda first taught us the importance of childlike wonder by showing us the absolute joy of viewing the world as if you are a child. Through this lens, time moves at a slower pace, gently trickling around our lives. She would visit in the summer when the rains fall heavily. When she heard the thick droplets on the tin roof, she would pull us outside to dance under their power. Our entire bodies became soaked in seconds, and our heavy feet made ripples in the mud. In this moment of freedom, our dancing bodies stood still in time. She taught us to play long games of Scrabble and to know the satisfaction of concentration. In the unscrambling of a magnificent seven-letter-word, we discovered the pleasure of our minds stretching to comprehend new knowledge. But we also learned to savor the boredom of these long games, and let our minds wander, contemplating the smallest things. This 80-year-old woman taught us that to live with childlike

wonder is to be present in every moment, to not linger in the past or think forward to the future. From her, we learned the simple meaning of the present moment, and it is only now that we see the power of this way of being.

As children, we let our minds and bodies wander, following a leaf in the stream or wallabies' prints in the mud. We were constantly learning new things and experiencing this world for the first time. With the enormity of this newfound knowledge, time seemed to move at a gentle pace. A tender tide of moments washed over us softly. In an unhurried rhythm, unaware of itself, each day was full of lessons and teaching, forming a tight weave of existence.

As we grew older, the momentum built. In the repetition and monotony of our adult lives, time has no place to slow. It moves so fast now, and we're carried by its torrent. It does not curl at the banks of new knowledge; it rushes forward and takes us with it. Looking back, we see that our great aunt Frieda always knew the secret of flowing with the tides of time. So now, we remember to practice this way of being. We wander, play, climb trees, explore, and sit quietly, approaching each moment with wonder and awe. Tracing the strands of a spider's web, we

understand the weave of being: the tangled and interlaced thread that constructs our lives. Like a map, the web circles us; each lesson or memory is marked by a new strand of silk. As children, the strands were tight in their weave, encompassing us closely. They were anchored by moments of meaning. As we age, these memories become further apart from one another. Every experience is a little less connected. But a distinct pattern emerges: a web of memories and lessons, woven by time.

If we are intentional with the days we are given, we can keep the weave of our existence tight. In the closeness of small moments, lessons, and continued learning, time becomes endless. So we fill our days with exploration and creativity. Life by the mountain is slow and repetitive, but in this, we are fulfilled by the immense expanse of possibility. We make paintings and sew gowns, write poems and sketch the seasons. We create for no reason but the perspective it brings. With time on our hands, we flow with the beauty of boredom and keep learning as a child does, finding deep reflection. Each day, each hardship, and each joy is a lesson that gives time a place to slow. We understand this life as a woven web of interlaced moments, and we create simple memories each day, worthy to remember.

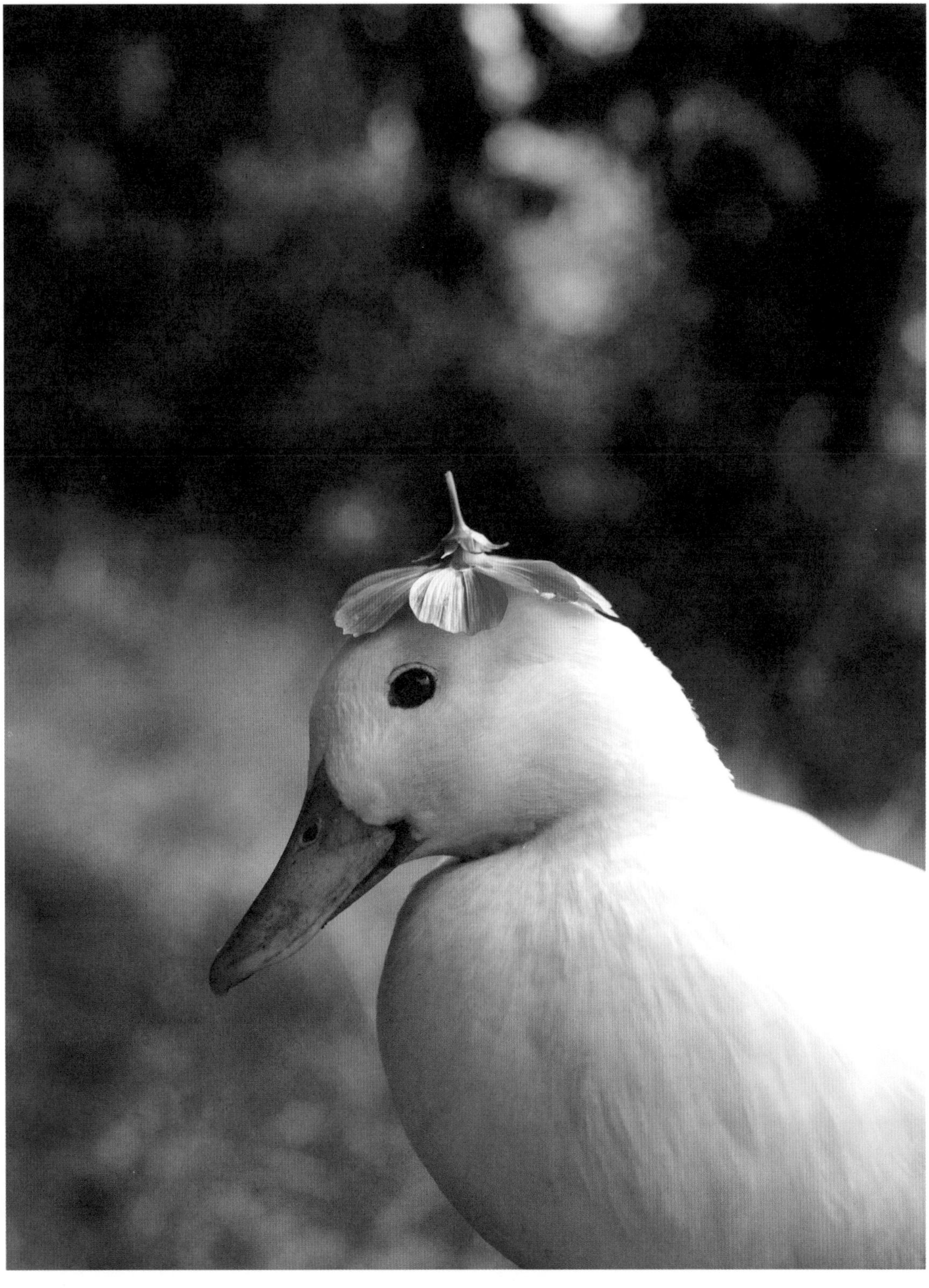

MONOTONY AND SPONTANEITY

The journeys of our lives meander. They don't follow linear paths but wander around obstacles, expand in the unknown, and reflect inward in the closeness of the everyday. Often, our days are simple and monotonous. We fix fences and care for the animals. But there is a magic to this humble way of being. Mindlessly free in menial tasks, we reflect—making connections between ourselves and the world. In our art studio, this introspection readily finds us. Between these tin walls, the past and future slip from view. Our minds are still, and our bodies are vessels for movement, hastily weaving each musing and reflection into our art.

JULIA: *A painting is a balance of freedom and careful composition, light and dark, stillness and movement. But it also requires a symmetry of mindsets. My strokes are both deliberate and aimless. I diligently work and then let myself fall into the rhythm of mindless creation. When I watch Anastasia sew, I see the same equilibrium of presence. I witness hours of meticulous pattern making, calculating, and planning, punctuated by moments of wild spontaneity. Just as I throw bold strokes of gestural color into my considered compositions, she fearlessly snips and tears the fabric, letting a moment of intuition be guided by hours of intention.*

We've come to see that our lives too, must follow this balance. We must find contemplation in the monotony of routine, and growth in the spontaneity of the unknown. In a grand tapestry, the warp is the tightly held strings, the stability on which the image is built. It is the simple act of repetition that holds the strength of our lives. But like any great tapestry, the weft is interlaced with color and texture, depth and meaning. Simplicity woven with complexity, monotony woven with spontaneity.

One autumn day, a group of us decided to hike all the way from home to our friend's house. She lives far across the mountains, and the only route to get there is a long road that winds almost to the ocean and then back up, deep into the rainforest. We held a map to the hills and understood that, as the wallabies do, we could walk instead. Over three mountains, one gorge, and a plateau; through a cave; and down the edge of a waterfall—we could trek to arrive at her front door. We set out, unsure of how long it would take or the exact route we would

follow. Our backpacks were too heavy, so we left behind our tents for clean water and swapped mattresses for cans of beans. It was this discomfort that we sought though: the simplicity of carrying only the tools for our survival.

We walked high into the bush and were swallowed by cliff faces and palm trees. The shifting light and curling streams were our only compass. Up above the caldera, we followed the mountain's edge for almost a day until we found a big cave under the escarpment. The archway of stone was carved like an eye that looked as if it were watching over the landscape. We climbed through the hollow and emerged to what felt like a new world. A waterfall flowed from high above, falling onto the rocks below. Its water moved softly, billowing in the wind. We kept climbing further, deep into the rainforest's center. Our minds drifted; our muscles ached. We gained a timeless awareness, sensing the strength of our small bodies carrying us across the landscape. The present moment was reduced to each step as we counted down the time until our next meal of cold beans or

patiently waited for the sun to rise over our beds made from collected grass.

After three days, we made it to our friend's house and were greeted with laughter and food. The comfort of warm meals and soft beds felt grander than we'd ever known. Our perspective had shifted in the unknown experiences of new landscapes and discomforts. Each morning's cup of tea, each day's tasks, and each night's somber sleep suddenly felt illuminated in the beauty of routine. Our lives became enchanted again in the magic of the everyday. When we finally returned to the animals, we saw how they greeted us with deep trust. They know that each morning and night, we will be there, caring for them—giving a scratch behind the ear or a tummy rub just the way they like it. In this consistency of care, the animals welcome us into their flock. They communicate with us, in senses, motions,

and sounds—with a glance of their eyes or a movement of their tails.

The ducks follow us everywhere we go, holding so much trust in their joyful waddle. If they waggle their tails, it means they are happy or excited. They bob their heads to show love when they flirt with each other or when they are reunited with an old friend. Some mornings, they fly to our shoulders and sit between our hair, their feathers molded to the shape of our necks. We hold them in our palms, and they look into our eyes and bob their heads passionately. In duck language, this means I *love you*. All at once, we understand this reciprocal love, the meaning of our care, and the beauty that routine brings. We see the unity and connection of care. The blessing of doing the same thing every day. The growth of new experiences and the need to weave harmonic monotony with intentional spontaneity.

CYCLES OF CARE

Like a wave standing still in time, the caldera surrounds us. The crater is a reminder of the towering volcano that once stood here. Around twenty-three million years ago it erupted, forming the valley we live in, the mountains we watch, and the soft creeks that move to the ocean.

Remnants from the eruption are hidden throughout the mountains: opals, quartz, and gold scatter the earth. We walk through the rainforest, down the edge of a steep gully. The shortcut winds below the palms and down steep rock faces. It is from here that we can see the cool flowing stream. At our feet, covered in fallen leaves and thick dirt, is a piece of wood that sits hard and cool in the depths of the forest. We uncover its solid surface and hold it in our hands to discover that it is a dense, heavy stone—a petrified piece of wood. After carrying it down the valley, we gently place it within the smooth curling creek, and mud disperses from ancient crevices, spreading like morning mist. We hold the fossil in our hands, tracing the suspended nodules, bark, and lines. Its stone feels impossible between our fingers. This tree would have grown before the volcano's eruption and then been petrified under volcanic ash. A frozen remnant of the Miocene forest sits within our grasp.

At the wood's core, tree rings spread. Each circle marks a completed cycle of the seasons. We count their rings and notice alternating thick lines between thin ones, indicating floods and droughts. Weather is illustrated by fast growth from plentiful rains or small weak circles from dry years. Each revolution permeates across its base, recording the tree's forgotten life. We imagine the trees

that have grown in our presence, and wonder what stories will be told within their rings. They will hold the scars of unprecedented fires and unthinkable floods, illustrating our changing climate between their flesh.

Our hands cusp the eternal stone, and we look at our own fingerprints that have lines stretching out like tree rings—a constant reminder of the cycles of our lives. With our fingers pressed against cold stone, we gain a timeless clarity; this glimpse of the past lets us understand the importance of our own present moment. We see our role within history, shaped by the past and guided by the future.

We sit still within the rippling stream as undulating water radiates around our bodies. The creek shines like opal, smoothly passing through worn boulders. Dragonflies circle us, creating halos from their movements. Cupping the water in our hands, droplets begin to fall, creating soft cyclic ripples that spread across the rainforest pool like a fingerprint.

We see our lives like the ripples between these rocks and the rings of the fossilized tree. Soft and shifting, they expand outward. Like time, they move only one way, uninterrupted in their circling movement. In these cyclical spirals we see the interwoven layers of history reflected: our ancestors etched within each ripple. Each generation is drawn within a new shimmering line. Undulations are formed by all that has been and all that will come. Molded by each other's rhythms, they spread through interconnected movements and fill the pool with their shapes.

We think of all those who have come before and all those who will come after us, understanding care as a boundless movement that radiates through time like a ripple. Our actions spread outward, shaping the future world. At the present moment, we have the power to shift its shape—each circle can become grander. The love, care, and action spreads. It heals.

AWARENESS PRACTICES

Be Present

Find presence and do not watch yourself through the warped illusions of time. You can be captured by the past and entangled between a web of memories. You can be misled by the future's song, allured by endless paths and possibilities. Be aware of the past, and know your duty to the future, but be present and feel the truth of each passing moment.

Routine

Find balance between spontaneity and monotony. Seek new experiences that foster growth, but rest in the understanding that routine holds stability. A fern glistens in spontaneous growth, with thousands of small tendrils filling its fronds. But if you look closely, each leaf is led by a distinct pattern, guided by a delicate routine.

A Hopeful Gaze

Find that hope is a lens to view the world. Through these eyes, see the invisible connections threaded through everything. Uncover the glistening ties that connect the flowers to the bees, the oceans to the clouds, and yourself to the earth. Let your life's actions thread hope into the world.

The Balance of Life

Find wholeness in balance. See that the moon is an illusion; it is not empty in darkness or full in light. Know that beyond its shifting phases, it is whole. Do not focus your view just on the illusions of lightness and dark, but find truth in the spaces between.

Vulnerability

Find that vulnerability and strength do not contend, but are held within each other's shadows. See that to be vulnerable takes great strength—each night the sun bows down and lets shadows engulf the earth. See that to be strong, you must be vulnerable—each day the darkness disperses and lets the day triumph.

Nurture Yourself, Others, and the Earth

Find that if you nurture yourself, you can be more nurturing to others. If you nurture others they can be more nurturing to the earth. See the cycles of care like undulating ripples moving with effortless grace. See connection, creativity, and care as our tools to heal the earth and to heal ourselves.

To Heal

Listen to the birds sing to their unhatched eggs,
they build a future within their nests.
See the fruit ripen for tomorrow's harvest,
their flesh is painted by imminence.
Feel the seeds between your fingers,
and envisage the garden that will grow.
Like nature, imagine a beautiful earth,
and find hope behind each new season's edge.

TRANSFORMATION

Nature is a force of transformation. She fills each expanse with a carefully attuned succession of growth. Her flourishing expands, shifts, adapts, and innovates, endlessly learning from the patterns of turbulence. In our time of stewarding this hopeful patch of earth, we have experienced moments of great turning that shaped us. We have stood on the front lines of climate disaster, and like nature, we have been transformed.

When the flood came, it scarred the earth with raging waters. No stone was left unturned, and the sound of shattering rocks echoed throughout the valley. We heard the earth's beating heart between crashing boulders. As the water receded, the pounding stopped, and the rainforest sat lifeless. In pain and fear, we crumbled too, but in our grief for the earth, we uncovered something powerful: we learned to love it more deeply. Our despair was formed by our love for the land, and in this bond grew boundless care. We felt nature as an extension of ourselves and knew our bodies as an element of her wholeness. We sensed all her pain and experienced all her wonder. In this deep connection, we found the art of living with nature.

ANASTASIA: *After the flood, I lay within the new creek's carved and hollowed stream, shaded by the dead quandong trees whose bark was stripped by the fierce waters. The stream encircled me; I was consumed between its power and vulnerability. Closing my eyes, I felt the water's familiar embrace against my skin. It held me how it always has. Between the crumbled boulders and falling leaves, I saw that even a broken earth is beautiful.*

Our experiences with disaster teach us to center ourselves and let the water pass us on either side, as we sit steady and calm like rocks in the stream. In this way of being, we do not dominate the landscape, but exist within the environment's complex wholeness. During our short time living with the land, we've seen the tilt of nature's balance before our own eyes. The earth's ingrained harmony is being fractured, and each year the imbalance deepens. The fires burn hotter, the storms are wilder, and we step further into the extremities of climate disaster. They shape us as they carve the landscape.

> **JULIA:** *After the fire, the earth was so still. I walked into the fallen forest between charred trees that were surrendered to the soil. No birds sung from the ashen branches. I looked closer to the charcoal and ash, and in its void, I saw glimpses of life. Vines curled around blackened trunks, holding them closely. Seedlings grew between old rotting logs. Wattles were sprouting in bare earth. Like us, these sprouts of change grew from charred ground.*

There were two paths that this growth could follow. In imbalance, the wattles could become a monoculture that smothers the ground where delicate ecosystems once flourished. Or, nurtured—the forest could find its way back to balance. In the ashes of the rainforest, we felt this same turning within ourselves. At first, our lives slipped into fear and disbelief, our understandings of safety and home pivoted on their axes. We saw only the path of imbalance before us. But in this moment of great change, we had a choice. From despair we turned to hope. We began to nurture the wounded forest back toward balance, and our fear shrunk in the face of action.

In a time shaped by climate disasters, we've learned to look to the balance of nature for guidance. Here we see the choice of devastation or regeneration. We do not approach crisis from the illusions of disbelief or despair—but from what holds the space in between: understanding. We hear the earth's cry for help, and in pain we listen. In the grounds from which our sorrow grows, we find the antidote to despair. It is found in our care. So we focus not just on the edge of our emotions, but on the depth. We feel fully in the hurt of the earth. We bathe in broken waters and wander through sinking ash. From this understanding grows our compassion. The earth is a part of us and we must nurture her back into wholeness. We don't stagnate in despair at her fractured harmony, but with action our movements create ripples. Our compassion compels us to act, and our care guides nature's path to balance.

EMPOWERMENT

Bare earth will always be the creative grounds of change. We see nature's resilience in each tendril of growth and inch of soil that teems with life. This reminds us to be the same and make the empty space of ourselves fertile, filled with the potential for growth.

Looking back, the times of our deepest loss were the times when we found the ability to transform within ourselves. When we lost our dad and returned to the rainforest, our hearts were pulled open in vulnerable uncertainty. Suddenly, our lives were inexplicably tied to nature—through storms, fires, droughts, and rains—what happened in this forest saw us survive or thrive, struggle or perish. But with our hearts wide and bare, we were sensitive not only to the pain, but to the beauty as well. By laying ourselves open, we found connection. Each small thing was adorned in growth and learning. More than anything else, we felt deeply. We felt love for the land and for ourselves, and from this, compassion grew. In care, we found a shifting of self, a courageous vulnerability. We found empowerment.

When we buried our dad, our whole community lowered him into the ground. We were surrounded by the people who he had fearlessly given his life to. Each day, he had offered his skills, his hands, and his labor to our neighbors and friends. They all knew the generosity of his laughter and the strength of his knowledge. Now, they held him in return.

The mountains surrounded us all, the afternoon light touched each friend and tree trunk. We looked over the farm, reminded that when a great tree falls, nature rushes to fill the hole in her canopy with growth and beauty. She is in a constant state of flux: never complete, always shifting, but whole in the perpetuity of change. Like nature, our community rushed to fill the hole our dad's passing had left. Our uncle helped us learn to build, and our friends returned Dad's generous love. All the seeds planted by our dad's giving had grown to become strong trees. A forest grew from his actions, and it held us, returning the knowledge and nestling new seeds under our skin. With the strength of this forest behind us, we took the responsibility of care into our grip. The land was our duty, and we bloomed in this knowledge. We saw that even the most disruptive forces could foster our growth. They compel us to feel fully in the hurt of the world and coalesce—filling a hole in the rainforest canopy with the strength of a thousand small trunks.

In the floods and fires, we always remembered this: that our grief is our strength. It is in our vulnerability that we relate, we connect to ourselves, the earth, and those around us—strengthening the innate links that tie us together. Understanding that our lives, our futures, and all our potential is tied together, we become one, united in collective care. There is courage in acceptance and joy in the hurt. Our grief comes from our love, and it is when we fearlessly face these things that we begin to care. We learn to heal and find wholeness as nature does. From this, a hopeful future emerges.

PURPOSE

Invisible connections and harmonious interactions are woven through the earth. Everything in nature has a purpose. Every beautiful thing is laced with meaning. The dragonflies' intricate fairy wings have hundreds of sensory neurons, letting them flutter with grace. The old, buttressed tree roots collect water for the dry season as the vines poetically climb through the canopy to reach the light. Between trunks and vines, these dragonflies feed on insects and are prey to the birds and fish. The strength of the vines create shelter and habitat while in the tree roots, insects and frogs breed. An invisible web connects every action and movement, every insect, tree, cloud, and stream.

We have found our purpose within this web. Discovering that like the dragonflies, trees, and vines, our actions resonate in the weave of the rainforest—we thread each moment with intention. Our fulfillment grows with every small action, and as they culminate, we discover that happiness is found in purpose. It is the simple feeling of making change with our hands. With simple contentment, we watch the work we do transform the landscape. We've found that happiness isn't a state of being, it is a fleeting feeling among a sea of emotions. Joy is dictated by passing moments, but purpose is deeper; it is the current that guides the ocean's waves, the birds that spread the forest's seeds, or the thread that weaves these moments together.

As the forest is simply a collection of growth, we understand that our lives are a collection of small moments. We see the seasons return again and again, watch the fog swirl through the valley, and the light fade off cliff faces. With gratitude, we eat food grown from the abundance of our hard work. In the radiating growth of the red cedars' shooting limbs, we see an affirmation that what we do here matters. We know our role on this earth.

> **ANASTASIA:** *After a hot day of weeding and planting, I dive into the lake and feel the soft water wash the dirt from my skin. I am immersed in each sense and sound. The kingfisher swoops for fish, and the waterlilies begin to close their buds as the afternoon fades. Around me are patches of change and beauty: the red cedars grow tall in the valley where we eliminated the competing weeds, the coolamons we planted have new branches spreading outward, and the goats roam happily in the forest above. The water's reflections cradle me, and within the landscape's embrace, I see the patches of change being sewn together. The stitches are our intention; they weave each small action into a grand tapestry. As the last golden light highlights each tree, I see a blanket of healing spread across the land.*

In the wonder of witnessing the land respond to our care, we feel welcome. We learn to belong as we sow seeds of hope and mend the earth. We feel what it means to care for the forest of an unknown future, and we walk through the landscape with pride. The change we sculpt resonates, and our actions spread seeds.

JULIA: *When I paint, I imagine a landscape of the future. I conjure a world of harmony while my strokes bring it into existence. The constant movement and energy of the rainforest guides me, and I paint its beauty with intention. It inspires me to capture what it means to live among this chaos and mutualism—symbiotic with the systems that enclose our lives. Stillness and movement, light and dark, wild color and empty space. Together, these dualities meld to create a fusion of fleeting moments. The combination of each small element makes a story of connection, honoring the greater beauty of this wonderful world and the meaning of our lives amid it.*

It is with honor that we care for this landscape and its future. We haven't counted how many trees we've planted, but the days spent with our hands in the soil are inscribed in our hearts. The act of care molds us. It extends throughout our lives. In the land, our skin, and our stories, we see the threads that weave us together. Layers of history are written between clouds, tree bark, and ripening fruit. But in the stories we tell, the saplings we plant, and the care that we continue, we see the threads of the future—an unwoven, imminent continuity. Our hands must carry on the weave. We must learn from the past while imagining a better future, using our presence to create a seamless tapestry of wholeness.

REGENERATION

There is an avocado tree on the highest hill of the farm. From here, you can watch over our whole little world. The tiny silhouettes of goats run from guava to persimmon tree, and wallabies bounce beside the lake. We climb into the comfort of the avocado tree's limbs for the best view of the setting sun. Like outstretched arms, branches reach in every direction. Between their palms, they hold eternal wisdom. This tree was planted 60 years ago, when our grandparents first moved to the rainforest. They started this journey with a single seed, and now we climb high within the branches of their vision. Through glistening leaves, we see the thousands of trees they planted and the regenerating ecosystems of the land. The touch of their care runs deep.

Further down the hill stands the tree that our parents planted, rooted with intention that transcends time. It cradles our bodies as we pick avocados from up high in the branches. The thousands of open leaves teach us to find knowledge within everything. Delicate flowers have begun to blossom for next season, and bees encircle them, collecting nectar for the hive. They teach us that to give and receive is to flourish with nature.

In the years since we became stewards of this land, we've watched ourselves transform and grow with the landscape. We eternally shift with each season, growing with the garden and moving to the stream's tide. When we first moved home, we planted an avocado tree below our parents' tree. It was a fragile sapling within our hands, but it grew through fires and floods and now stands taller than us. Its leaves glisten in the afternoon light, and tiny

avocado buds fill its branches. It sits so proudly, spreading its leaves to the sun.

Now, the three trees descend down the hill with deep twirling roots reaching far below the surface. Our roots are entangled with the trees planted by those before us. They teach us to search deep within, and feel our ancestors' knowledge flowing like nutrients through taproots.

The generations of care expand outward. With a shared purpose, we tend the soil and the forest as our grandparents and parents once did. Our tree will drop fruit, rolling its seeds down the hill and into the fertile grounds of the future. In the three trees and the restoring rainforest, we see the impact of a simple action, radiating through time. When our grandparents planted the old avocado tree so many years ago, they did not imagine their action of hope would continue for generations to come. They planted with courage, holding the power to imagine a better future. From this, a momentum of care built. In their small acts of faith, they grew a bountiful forest.

The collective knowledge of three generations of nature's lessons guides us to restore, to renew, and to heal. The gift of fruit acts as a spark of light in this world, a shining reminder that the smallest actions can make great change. They can spread through us like whispers, igniting our impulse to grow toward balance, to give back, and to work as one. We watch the grand avocado tree and see that each leaf grows with the silent knowledge of the whole tree. These leaves are guided by a great purpose and work collectively toward growth.

As we sit below the chain of trees planted by those before us, we understand that we are daughters of the earth. We are all born from nature's systems, etched with the truth of the sun, the stars, and the shifting seasons. Moving to the pace of the earth, we see that our lives are entangled with the cycles of its wholeness. Ripening fruit grows with hopeful seeds, teaching us that we must become mothers to a new earth. We must imagine a beautiful world and plant its seeds into existence.

HOPE

Glimpses of light pass between the canopy, and leaves outstretch in its presence. In the rainforest, each fern, vine, leaf, and tendril shifts with intention. The tallest bunyas and red cedars catch the light, casting great shadows below. On the forest floor the brightest ferns, palms, and mosses grow in darkness. Each tree stands solid on buttressed roots, held by ancient vines that connect everything. When one of these great trees falls, the forest falls with it. Suddenly, the forceful light pushes into the depths of the rainforest where bare earth is broken by ripped tree roots, raw and vulnerable.

In a collapsing environment, we look at this bare earth, devoid of any life. We see our world reflected in broken roots and pale soil. The earth is fractured, and the great trees are falling. Our hands hold the tools of their destruction. But in our palms, there are also the seeds of restoration. The guidance of how to plant these seeds lies in nature's wisdom.

In the rainforest, macaranga are the first seeds that sprout from shattered soil. They climb toward the sun, their towering stems and immense leaves quickly shading the disturbed earth once again. Mimicking the balance of the fallen forest, they create a habitat for the seeds of slow-growing grand trees that take root in their shade. It can take thousands of years for the biodiversity of a rainforest to recover, but on the edge of destruction, the macaranga grows with ceaseless hope.

In their intentional growth and generous shade, these seedlings protect the forest. It is their purpose to imagine a better world for those who will come after them. Like the macaranga, our hands must cusp the light and shape it for those to come. In boundless hope, we cast protective shade and nurture growth in the most barren land. We will sow seeds of hope and cultivate a forest of the future.

But a macaranga sapling does not act alone—one singular seed would not be able to shield the earth. Instead, countless seeds awaken from dormancy, catalyzed by destruction. They have evolved for this purpose. In a thousand small sprouts, they heal a patch of ground, joining their shade in a protective blanket of care. Their collective purpose creates a wave of growth, and the slow-growing giants of the rainforest sprout in its wake.

In nature's extraordinary resilience lies the answers to our future. Together, we can rise from broken earth like stirring saplings, activated in care. The hopeful seeds of a better earth lie dormant under our skin. They awaken in the knowledge of our past and the vision of a wondrous future. This potential to nurture is within us all. From dormancy to action, we can join the current of nature's unwavering ability to heal. It will carry us home.

The land we live on has been protected for thousands of years by its Traditional Owners, the Arakwal and Minjungbal people of the Bundjalung Nation. Held in this continuous care of Country is the potential of a regenerative future. When we look to Indigenous knowledge, we see a way of living founded in a deep connection to and care of the land. It is here that answers lie. All around the world, First Nations peoples safehold the biodiversity of our earth—seeds, ecosystems, and water cycles are protected through their knowledge and care. If we listen, it is this wisdom that will guide our path to a beautiful future lived harmoniously with the earth.

Acknowledgments

This book was made by many hands, hearts, and minds. To tell this story is an immense honor, and we are eternally grateful to everyone who helped bring our vision of hope into being.

We'd like to begin by thanking the people of the hills: our neighbors, friends, and family. The words and images of this book have been forged in the nurturing support of this community who held us when we needed them most. We would never have been able to navigate this journey without your strength.

To our mum, whose unwavering courage has always guided us. We hold each glistening truth you've taught us in our hearts. The photographs that fill these pages eternalize our bond—taken from your artful perspective, they will always hold the feeling of the three of us and the mountains. We treasure these ethereal compositions, captured through the gaze of motherly love.

To our brother, Riley, who fights fires and gives with selfless bravery. Thank you for teaching us to traverse this caldera and appreciate each hill and stone. To our uncle Adam, for his friendship and guidance; from him, we learned to build with graceful diligence. To our cousin Nikita Vanderbyl, who also holds the skills of the axe— thank you for your knowledge. To each old farmer and new friend who taught us to garden, farm, and see the power of storytelling.

Most of all, we are grateful to our online community that spreads like threads from this little rainforest farm into the world. This global community that came together as we told our story gives us hope more than anything else. We have found friends in every corner of the earth, united in the wonder of our extraordinary world. Without this endless support, we would never have had the privilege of sharing our story and our love of this earth.

Thank you to our wonderful editor, Alexander Rigby, who saw our vision and believed in us from the very beginning. It was during the 2022 flood disaster that Alex first suggested the idea of a book of hope. The flood revealed to us how vulnerable and resilient the earth truly is, and with clarity, we saw our duty—to share the beauty of nature and why it is so important to protect it. Among the devastation, we climbed through thick mud and landslides to the highest hill where we were able to get just enough reception to reply with passion: we were ready to write this book! Thank you, Alex, for the depth you offered to this vast project and your care through everything. Many thanks to the wonderful team at DK and Penguin Random House, especially Joanna Price for your design skills and intricate touch with each photograph and artwork.

During the time of writing this book, we recovered from climate disasters and loss, but were galvanized in the strength of a community joining in togetherness. We lost significant people from the generations before us—our Grandma Hazel, Great-Tante Frieda, and Great-Tante Liesbeth. These women taught us to be artists and innovators; they were graceful carers, and as they left we felt the responsibility of the earth pass into our hands. Their wisdom and the power of hopeful action guides our way.

We are indebted to the deep knowledge of nature, our community, and supporters for shaping this book into what it is today. The teachings of each animal, insect, plant, and microbe are woven through these stories. Every aspect of our selves are imprinted in these pages; they hold the essence of our beings and of the rainforest. We still have much to learn but feel endlessly honored to be on this journey alongside you all.

With heartfelt gratitude we would like to thank our readers and supporters—the big community of lovers of the earth who without your friendship, none of this would be possible. Together, we are creating a world filled with joy and hope; we are storytelling a wondrous future into existence.

Index

Sisters Anastasia and Julia Vanderbyl are the artists and farmers behind
Mother the Mountain, an environmental platform that has amassed a
devoted fan base of over 2 million followers. Through film, art, and
photography, they document their journey of restoring the rainforest,
caring for animals, and living with nature, inspiring their audience to
celebrate and protect the beauty of the natural world. Anastasia is a fashion
designer who works with regenerative practices to create ethereal pieces,
and Julia is an internationally exhibited painter whose work examines
the interplay of human and environment. They both live and grow on
Bundjalung Country on the East Coast of Australia, where they care for a
regenerative farm previously stewarded by their parents and grandparents.